TWO JEWISH PLAYS

Gotthold Lessing

TWO JEWISH PLAYS

THE JEWS
NATHAN THE WISE

Translated and introduced by
Noel Clark

OBERON BOOKS
LONDON

These translations first published in 2002 by Oberon Books Ltd.
Electronic edition published in 2013

Oberon Books Ltd.
521 Caledonian Road, London N7 9RH
Tel: 020 7607 3637 / Fax: 020 7607 3629
e-mail: info@oberon.books.com
www.oberonbooks.com

Reprinted in 2011

A catalogue record for this book is available from the British
Library.

PB ISBN: 978-1-84002-208-7

E ISBN: 9781783194025

Cover design: Andrzej Klimowski

eBook conversion by Replika Press PVT Ltd, India.

Visit www.oberonbooks.com to read more about all our books
and to buy them. You will also find features, author inter-
views and news of any author events, and you can sign up for
e-newsletters so that you're always first to hear about our new
releases.

Contents

Introduction

'We Must Be Friends!'

The cosy Victorian stereotype of our German cousins as a nation of amiable, pipe-smoking intellectuals, musicians, artists and dreamers (with a stiffening of jackbooted Prussians strutting about off-stage) did not long survive the onset of the twentieth century. Two world wars and the Holocaust – stamped 'Made in Germany' – took care of that. But the world moves on. So must we.

It is, however, a fact that the substitute stereotype bequeathed to Europe and the world by Adolf Hitler and his henchmen dies hard. Every so often, old newsreel footage of swastikaed Stukas dive-bombing defenceless cities, let alone shots of nude corpses piled higgledy-piggledy in the death camps, rekindle our revulsion at what all of us – Germans included – must nowadays do our best to regard as an appalling, incomprehensible, yet transient aberration. The alternative would be to despair of humanity altogether. At the beginning of the third millennium, that is hardly an option.

Fifty years on, we find ourselves not merely neighbours but partners and allies of a new and powerful, democratic Germany, reunited barely a decade ago. But the restoration of mutual trust and confidence between peoples is a slow business. The crimes of the Nazi era will doubtless continue to revolt, frighten and baffle successive generations of young Europeans, not least the Germans themselves, for decades to come.

Meanwhile, it might be well for all of us to aid the restorative work of historical perspective by reminding ourselves that Germany was once the seed-bed of thinkers, philosophers, writers, musicians, artists and scientists, who contributed richly to the advance of European civilisation.

Sceptics, of course, may ask whether any of them sensed where Germans in particular and mankind in general might be heading. Did nobody raise the alarm? If so, to what effect?

Though his name is familiar to few of us these days, Gotthold Ephraim Lessing (1729–1781) was a towering figure in the history of German theatre. Playwright, philosopher, critic and polemicist, Lessing was Germany's leading contributor to the eighteenth-century wave of Enlightenment, then permeating Europe from Britain and France. In years to come, the British historian and statesman, Lord Macaulay, was to rate Lessing 'the first critic in Europe'. Another admirer was the distinguished Scottish philosopher and translator of German literature, Thomas Carlyle, while the German-Jewish poet, Heinrich Heine, described Lessing as 'a soldier in the Liberation War of humanity'.

One of Lessing's major achievements was to free German theatre from the thralldom of the French neo-classical plays of Corneille and Racine. By his example as a playwright and his exhortation as a critic, Lessing induced aspiring German dramatists to model their plays instead on the realistic blank verse dramas of England's Shakespeare. Perhaps best remembered by his compatriots as the author of *Minna von Barnhelm* – one of the few comedies in German to rank as a classic – Lessing is often credited with laying the foundations of modern German drama with his realistic 'social tragedies', notably *Miss Sara Sampson*.* Most of his plays – however innovative when written – are nowadays mainly of literary-historical interest. There are, however, two major exceptions: *The Jews* (1749) and *Nathan the Wise* (1779).

These two plays contain the essence of Lessing's rational humanist philosophy: a passionate plea for tolerance, reason, common sense and respect, not only between Christians and Jews but for all humanity, regardless of race, creed or colour. Not surprisingly, these two works – the first written when the author was in his twenties and the second, only two years before his death – were banned by the Nazis and restored to classic status only after the defeat of Hitler's Reich.

The Jews, a longish one-acter, is a hybrid of comedy and earnest polemic, born of youthful outrage: a precocious denunciation of anti-semitism, as much for its 'stupidity' as for the inhumanity of all racial prejudice. Both the theme and presentation were highly

---

* *Sara,* translated by Ernest Bell and *Minna von Barnhelm,* translated by Anthony Meech, published by Absolute Classics, an imprint of Oberon Books Ltd., ISBN 0 948230 29 0

controversial for the period. Lessing was criticised, among other things, for exaggerating beyond belief both the virtues of the play's Jewish hero and the villainy of the Christian highwaymen. Nevertheless the play is thought by some to have helped bring about a slight, if temporary, reduction in some of the disabilities suffered by Prussia's Jewish minority. In 1998, a staged reading in English of this long neglected comedy, at the Shakespeare Globe Theatre's Education Centre in London, demonstrated the play's ability to make a modern audience laugh and reflect – uneasily.

One of Lessing's most perceptive German biographers, the contemporary writer and critic, Dieter Hildebrandt*, quotes the words which Lessing puts into the mouth of Martin Krumm, the murderous Bailiff on the Baron's estate: 'Just as well I'm not King, or there wouldn't be one – not one of them – left alive! ...I was once at a fair. The very thought of that fair makes me want to poison every damned Jew alive – if only I could!'

Were these no more than the words of a villain in an eighteenth century play?, Hildebrandt asks, adding, 'If so, where did all the Martin Krumms come from in 1933 – and the mobs of Martin Krumms on "Crystal Night"?' That was the night – November 9/10, 1938 – when Nazi-organised mobs burned and looted synagogues and Jewish shops all over Germany. 'And where,' Hildebrandt wrote in 1979, 'are the Martin Krumms hiding today?'

Lessing came from a strict Lutheran background. His father, a pastor, was bitterly disappointed when his son, after showing early promise of academic brilliance, chose to devote his talents and his life to the theatre and journalism. Lessing's first ambition, as he confided in a letter to his parents, was to become a German Molière. There was no reason, he argued, why a Christian should not be able to write good comedies. However, although he apparently remained a God-fearing man, Lessing soon lost patience with the dogmas of conventional Christianity.

As his creative and critical powers developed and matured, so did the strength of his opposition to all forms of intolerance,

---

* *Lessing – Biographie einer Emanzipation* by Dieter Hildebrandt, published by Hanser Verlag, Munich.

racism, discrimination and bigotry – religious as well as political. For Lessing, unorthodoxy became almost a creed in itself, a personal system of philosophy which coloured both his private and public life. From 1754 onwards, for example, one of his closest friends and fellow campaigners for religious tolerance was the outstanding Jewish scholar of the day, Moses Mendelssohn, who first won Lessing's esteem by his stout defence of *The Jews* against hostile critics.

Though himself a Saxon born and bred, it was typical of Lessing not to let the traditional enmity between Saxony and Prussia prevent him from spending five years as secretary to a Prussian general. Lessing maintained impishly that he enjoyed arguing the Saxon case when in the company of Prussians and vice versa.

Despite early and enduring fame as a dramatist, critic and thinker, Lessing seems never to have made much money. For most of his relatively short but amazingly prolific life, he was plagued by 'cash-flow' problems, accentuated by his generosity to impoverished relatives and friends, and his own penchant for gambling. He was already forty-two when he became engaged to Eva Koenig, the widow of a merchant. It was another five years, however, before he felt able to marry her, having at last secured a steady appointment as chief librarian at the Duke of Braunschweig's vast research library in Wolfenbüttel – then a magnet for men of learning from all over Europe. His happy marriage, however, was blighted within a year by the death of his wife, followed by that of their only son.

Sooner or later, a polemicist as talented and irrepressible as Lessing was bound to fall foul of the censors. In 1778, his spirited defence of a free-thinker brought him into public conflict with a leading Lutheran divine, Chief Pastor Goetze of Hamburg. Lessing had previously been exempt from censorship but this privilege was now abruptly cancelled by his patron the Duke and he was forbidden to publish any further religious polemics. Lessing let it be known that he would resume the struggle for religious tolerance and freedom of thought from what he called his 'former pulpit', namely, the stage.

The following year, Lessing published his masterpiece *Nathan the Wise*, a five-act blank-verse drama, later to become one of the most translated plays in the German language. Sub-titled 'A dramatic poem', possibly to confuse the censors, the play's action was set in Jerusalem at the time of the Third Crusade (1192). The choice of both place and protagonists enabled the author to focus on the highly controversial topics of religion, race and human relations without seeming to act in open defiance of the ban.

Three of the world's great religions are personified in the play – Judaism by the wise Jewish merchant, Nathan; Islam by the Turkish Sultan Saladin, his sister Sittah and a Dervish; Christianity – often with brutal frankness – by a Templar Knight, the extremist Patriarch of Jerusalem, a pious lay-brother and Recha, ostensibly Nathan's daughter, but in reality his ward, and her companion, Daya – two Christians in a Jewish household.

Into what might be described as a philosopher's fairytale, Lessing poured a lifetime's reflection on the way of the world and man's relationship with his fellow-creatures and with God. True to the ethos of the Enlightenment era which he helped to inspire, Lessing's purpose was educational. The play, though far from being a tract, is meant to make us think while observing the evolution of the main characters as human beings in the course of a quest for the truth about themselves and the situation in which they find themselves.

Lessing once wrote that if God were to offer him a choice between truth and the quest for truth, he would opt for the latter. He disputed the claim of any one religion or political system to purvey incontrovertible truth here on earth. Absolute truth, he judged to be the prerogative of God alone and unattainable by man, whose duty and purpose in life, nonetheless, was to strive towards it in concert with the rest of humanity.

By this process of search and research, powered by the free exchange of thoughts and opinions among individuals encouraged to think for themselves, knowledge would spread, mutual respect and understanding would grow and civilisation be advanced. Or so it appeared to the luminaries of the Enlightenment era. Dare we think differently today?

The quest for truth, then, is one strand of *Nathan the Wise*. Another, no less significant, is the importance of friendship between individuals divided by race or creed – friendship seen as a prerequisite for rational discussion and the fruitful exchange of views, as well as the most effective means of transcending barriers to progress imposed by ignorance and inherited prejudice. In *The Jews*, Lessing's Jewish hero, known throughout as the Traveller, defines true friendship as 'a spontaneous inclination of the soul' towards a fellow human being. This thought is further developed in *Nathan the Wise*. During an outspoken debate with the Christian Templar, the Jew Nathan exclaims:

> We must, we simply must be friends! You may
> Despise my people to your heart's content;
> We neither of us, Templar, chose our race!
> Are we our people? What does 'people' mean?
> Are Jews and Christians rather Jews and Christians
> Than fellow-humans? Haven't I found in you
> A man of whom, it is enough to say:
> 'This is a man!'

Finally, the Templar echoes the words of Nathan:

> We must – we must be friends!

and

> We are already!

is Nathan's reply. Similarly, in the celebrated 'Ring Fable' scene, in order to avoid giving possibly fatal offence to the Moslem Sultan Saladin, Nathan side-steps the Sultan's demand to know which of the three great religions represented is the true faith. Instead of answering the loaded question, he adapts a fable borrowed from Boccaccio: the story of three sons whose loving father bequeaths to each a ring. Of the three rings, however, only one is the father's original, the other two being identical copies. Since the true ring alone has the power to make its possessor pleasing to God, each brother must therefore trust in the presumed power of his own ring and behave accordingly. Saladin, greatly impressed by the wisdom of the Jew, dismisses him with the words: 'Go, Nathan, go! But always be my friend!' For Lessing, as for Nathan, what counts is not the observance of religious ritual and dogma, but the performance of 'good' deeds, especially those which result from man's submission to

God's will. Nathan's immediate reaction to the burning to death by Christians of his wife and seven sons in a twelfth century holocaust is to rage against God for three days and nights, while swearing to hate all Christendom for ever.

But reason gradually gained the upper hand.
Its gentle voice proclaimed, 'Yet God exists!
That, too, was his decree. So brace yourself!'

Bracing himself, Nathan undertakes, for the sake of friendship and the assertion of his own humanity under God, to rear an abandoned Christian infant, Recha, as his own daughter, imparting no sectarian dogma but teaching her only to believe in God and distinguish between good and evil. In Lessing's day, as in our own, there was evidence that a bigoted sectarian interpretation of 'the will of God' could happily embrace even the slaughter of innocents in a 'religious' cause. It is the Patriarch of Jerusalem in Lessing's play who repeatedly insists 'The Jew must burn!'

The strength of *Nathan the Wise* lies not in its cleverly contrived though ludicrously improbable scenario which ends with the main characters, except for Nathan himself, discovering they are blood relatives and dissolving in mutual embrace. What gives the play eternal validity is the sincerity of its message, conveyed in polished dialogue, spiced with humour and satire. It may not be easy for us nowadays to share the optimistic 'mindset' of the Enlightenment era – or even to accept that two lovers, suddenly made aware of being brother and sister, could so readily forego passion for 'friendship', without, at the very least, a show of wild despair.

Nevertheless, in Lessing, we can recognize a mind at work whose uncertainties, hopes and fears anticipate and often chime with our own. Lessing himself was not over-confident about the long-term impact of his play. He wrote, 'It may well be that my *Nathan*, by and large, will have little effect, should it be staged, which indeed may never happen...' The play was first performed in Berlin two years after his death but it was not until 1802, in an adaptation by the dramatist Schiller and praised by Goethe, that *Nathan*'s place in German repertory was secure – or seemed to be.

Even so, there were always those – including the philosopher

Kant – who could not stomach the notion of a play with a Jew as hero. There were periods, too, when the play, as Dieter Hildebrandt, remarks, fell out of favour with the German public. At such times, Hildebrandt observes, things happened in Germany 'similar to what Nathan the Jew himself experienced and barely managed to survive.'

The moral of Lessing's visionary drama, however, is not for young Germans only to contemplate in relation to a past not of their making. In the world at large, most obviously in the Middle East, Africa, the Balkans, the North of Ireland – and marginally in our own backyard – racism, discrimination, extremism, 'ethnic cleansing' and blind sectarian strife continue to blight the lives of millions. Lessing is talking to all of us. The challenge of Nathan's appeal, 'We must be friends!' has still to be met, which is reason enough to give him a fresh hearing at the outset of what one can only hope – yet again – may prove to be a new age of more enduring Enlightenment.

Noel Clark
London
February 2002

THE JEWS

a comedy in one act

Characters

MICHAEL STAB
(Michael Stich)

MARTIN CROOK
(Martin Krumm)

A TRAVELLER

CHRISTOPHER
his servant

The BARON

A YOUNG LADY
his daughter

LISETTE
her chamber maid

This translation of *The Jews*, commissioned by Globe Theatre Education, was first presented as a staged reading in August 1998, with the following cast:

MICHAEL STAB, Iain Stirland

MARTIN CROOK, Nick Wilton

TRAVELLER, Jasper Britton

CHRISTOPHER, Lee Johnson

BARON, Paul Darrow

YOUNG LADY, Lara Bobroff

LISETTE, Sophie Greenlees

Co-ordinated by Peter Benedict

Translator's Note

The scene is the Baron's estate in Prussia. At the time of the action – the middle of the eighteenth century – there were said to be 2093 Jewish families living in the state. It was forbidden by law for any Jew to employ a Christian as a servant. Mixed marriage between Christians and Jews was also forbidden.

Scene 1

MICHAEL STAB and MARTIN CROOK.

CROOK: Michael Stab, you're an idiot!

STAB: And you're another, Martin Crook!

CROOK: Let's face it: prize-idiots, the pair of us. What difference would it have made to kill one more?

STAB: But how could we have planned it better? Both of us were well disguised... We had the coachman on our side, hadn't we? How could we help a stroke of bad luck? Haven't I said hundreds of times: blast our luck! Without it, you can't even be a successful villain!

CROOK: Thinking it over the morning after, seems to me we've barely escaped the noose for an extra day or two.

STAB: What's the noose got to do with it? If every thief got hanged the gallows would need to be a lot thicker on the ground. There's hardly a gibbet every two miles. And where you *do* see one, it's usually vacant. Wouldn't be surprised myself if their lordships, the judges, had them taken down out of politeness. What purpose do they serve? None, save at best to give the likes of us something to wink at in passing.

CROOK: Personally, I don't even wink. My father and my grandfather were both strung up. What more could I ask for? I'm not ashamed of my parents.

STAB: But those good folk will be ashamed of *you*. It's a long time since you did anything to prove yourself their real and rightful son.

CROOK: You think that's any reason to let our master off lightly? I'll certainly take my revenge on that blasted stranger for snatching such a juicy titbit from under our noses. That's going to cost him his watch... Look out, here he comes! You clear off quick! Leave it to me! This calls for my expert touch!

STAB: Don't forget we're going shares – fifty-fifty!

(*Exit STAB.*)

Scene 2

MARTIN CROOK and the TRAVELLER.

CROOK: (*Aside.*) I'll play stupid... (*Aloud.*) Martin Crook, sir, at your service! I'm the appointed manager of the estate – the owner's bailiff.

TRAVELLER: No doubt, my friend. But do you happen to have seen my servant?

CROOK: I'm sorry, no. But I have had the honour of hearing your worthy self spoken of so highly that I'm delighted now to enjoy the honour of making your acquaintance. I understand that you extricated our master yesterday evening, while travelling, from a most dangerous...er – danger. As I cannot fail to delight in my master's good fortune, I am delighted –

TRAVELLER: I can guess what you want. You wish to thank me for coming to the aid of your master.

CROOK: Quite right! That's it exactly...

TRAVELLER: You are an honest fellow –

CROOK: I am indeed. Honesty's the best policy in the long run.

TRAVELLER: It's a great pleasure to me to know that so trivial a favour has won me the esteem of so many good souls. Your recognition is more than enough reward for what I did. I was impelled to act simply by love of my fellow-humans. Indeed, I would be perfectly content were my action to be seen as no more or less than my duty. You are too generous, my friends, in thanking me for a deed which, I am sure, you would have performed with no less zeal on my behalf, had I found myself in similar peril. Can I be of some further service to you?

CROOK: Far be it from me to burden you, sir. I have a farm-hand to do my bidding if need be. But I would very much like to know what happened. Where was it? Were there many villains involved? Did they mean to kill our good master, or did they simply want to steal his cash – the one being doubtless preferable to the other.

TRAVELLER: I'll give you a brief account of the whole affair.

It must have happened about an hour away from here.
The robbers had ambushed your master in a defile. I was
travelling the selfsame route when his fearful cries for help
brought me and my servant galloping to the rescue.

ROOK: Well, I never –

TRAVELLER: I found him in an open carriage –

CROOK: Dear, oh dear!

TRAVELLER: Two fellows in disguise –

CROOK: Disguised, you say? What next!

TRAVELLER: Yes! They had already overpowered him.

CROOK: My poor master!

TRAVELLER: Whether they had a mind to kill him, or
simply to tie him up, in order to rob him the more safely
– that I don't know.

CROOK: They'd surely have wanted to kill him, the godless
rogues!

TRAVELLER: I wouldn't go so far as to say that, for fear of
doing them an injustice.

CROOK: Oh, take my word for it, they meant to kill him, all
right! I know… I'm certain of it!

TRAVELLER: How could you possibly be? But never mind.
No sooner did the robbers catch sight of me, than they
dropped their booty and fled full-tilt into the nearby
bushes. I fired my pistol at one of them. But it was already
too dark, or the fellow too far away. I very much doubt I
hit him.

CROOK: No, you didn't hit him.

TRAVELLER: You know that for a fact?

CROOK: It's just my opinion, seeing as how it was already
dark. As I understand it, one can't take proper aim in the
dark.

TRAVELLER: I can't tell you how grateful your master was
to me. A hundred times he called me his saviour and
invited me to return with him to his estate. I only wish
my circumstances allowed me to spend longer with such a
congenial host. However, I have to resume my journey this
very day. In fact, that's why I'm looking for my servant.

CROOK: Then don't spend too long with me. But, if you can

spare another moment or two, there was something else
I wanted to ask you... Yes – the robbers – tell me – what
did they look like? How did they get away? They were
disguised, weren't they? What as?

TRAVELLER: No doubt, your master will say they were Jews.
They had beards, it's true. But they spoke with the normal
peasant accent of this region. If they were in disguise, as
I believe, the dusk, of course, was to their advantage. I
can't understand, though, how Jews could make the roads
hereabouts unsafe, since this country tolerates so few of
them.

CROOK: It's true, though. I'm also convinced they were Jews.
You probably don't know the godless rabble all that well.
However many there be, they're all – without exception
– cheats, thieves and highwaymen. That's why they're also
a people cursed by God. Just as well I'm not King, or there
wouldn't be one – not one of them – left alive. God protect
all decent Christians from people of their sort! If God
himself didn't hate them, how come – only a short while
ago, in the Breslau disaster, almost twice as many Jews as
Christians perished? Our local pastor very wisely pointed
that out in his last sermon. It's as if they were listening and
at once decided to take their revenge on our master. My
dear sir, if you seek grace and good fortune in this world,
best be on your guard against Jews. Shun them! Worse than
the plague!

TRAVELLER: Would to God it were only the common
people who said such things!

CROOK: Let me give you an example: I was once at the Fair.
The very thought of that Fair makes me want to poison
every damned Jew alive – if only I could! In the crush,
one man had his handkerchief, another his snuff box, yet
another his watch and Lord knows what else – whipped
out of his pocket. They're nifty as weasels – when it comes
to theft; even nimbler than our old school-master ever was
on the organ. This is how they operate. First, they press up
against you, the way I'm doing now with you –

TRAVELLER: Only a shade more politely, my friend –

CROOK: Just let me show you how it's done. He's stood there beside you – see? Then, into your watch-pocket goes his hand – swift as a flash.

(*Instead of the watch pocket, CROOK puts his hand into the TRAVELLER's coat pocket and seizes his snuff box.*)

But he's that quick about it, you'd swear his hand was still going in when it's already on its way out. If he mentions a snuff box, you may be sure he's after your watch – and vice-versa.

(*CROOK now tries quite carefully to steal the TRAVELLER's watch but is caught in the act.*)

TRAVELLER: Hey, there! Go easy! What's that hand of yours up to now?

CROOK: You can see for yourself, sir, what sort of a clumsy pickpocket I'd make! If a Jew made a grab like that, you could certainly say goodbye to your watch. However, since I'm beginning to bore you, I'll take the liberty of excusing myself with my best respects, while remaining for life indebted to you for your generous action – your most obedient servant, Martin Crook, bailiff of this most noble estate.

TRAVELLER: On your way then! Off you go!

CROOK: Just don't you forget what I've been telling you about those Jews. They're nothing but a godless race of thieves!

Scene 3

The TRAVELLER.

TRAVELLER: I wouldn't be surprised if – stupid as he is, or pretends to be – that fellow isn't a more wicked scoundrel than any Jew ever. If a Jew cheats, nine times out of ten, likely as not, he's been driven to it by a Christian. I doubt whether many Christians could claim they'd always dealt honestly with a Jew. Yet they're surprised when a Jew tries to repay them in kind. If trust and decency are to prevail between two peoples, both must contribute equally thereto. But how can that be, when one of them regards it as a religious principle – almost a meritorious act – to persecute the other? All the same –

Scene 4

The TRAVELLER and CHRISTOPHER.

TRAVELLER: Why does it always take an hour to find you when you're needed?

CHRISTOPHER: You must be joking, sir. I can't be in more than one place at any given time, can I? So is it my fault if you don't always go to the place where I am? You're always certain to find me where I happen to be.

TRAVELLER: Indeed! You're not staggering, are you? Now I understand why you're so witty. Do you have to get drunk this early in the day?

CHRISTOPHER: What do you mean 'drunk'? I've barely started drinking as yet. On my word of honour, apart from two good bottles of local wine, a couple of brandies and a bread roll, I've not touched a drop today. I'm still completely sober.

TRAVELLER: I can tell that by the look of you. My advice to you, as a friend, is to eat twice as much.

CHRISTOPHER: Excellent advice! I shall not fail in my duty to consider that an order to be at once obeyed, as you shall see.

TRAVELLER: If you know what's good for you, you'll go now, saddle the horses and load our luggage. I want to be on the road again by noon.

CHRISTOPHER: Since you've just advised me in jest to eat a second breakfast, why should I imagine you're now in earnest? You seem bent on pulling my leg today. Is it the young lady who's put you in such a good mood? She's a very sweet-natured child. But she needs to be just a little – a wee bit older, sir, don't you think? Unless the girl has reached a certain stage of ripeness –

TRAVELLER: Go and do what I told you.

CHRISTOPHER: Now, you're becoming serious again. Nevertheless, I'll wait till you've given the order three times. This is a very important matter. Perhaps you were in too much of a hurry. I've always been used to allowing my gentlemen time to reflect. Consider carefully whether we ought so speedily to abandon a place where we're being so well looked after. We arrived only yesterday. Moreover, our host is eternally indebted to us and so far we've enjoyed only one of his suppers and a breakfast.

TRAVELLER: I can't stand your boorish manners! If you want to be a good servant, you must learn to make less fuss.

CHRISTOPHER: Very good, sir! Now you're starting to moralise, which is a sign you're getting angry. Just calm down. I'll go at once –

TRAVELLER: You're not in the habit of thinking things over. The service we did this gentleman forfeits the right to be termed a good deed, the moment we appear to expect some recognition in return. Strictly speaking, I shouldn't even have allowed myself to be invited here. To have gone to the aid of a stranger, without an ulterior motive, is cause for great satisfaction. The stranger, himself, would later have blessed us in his thoughts, even more fervently than he now does in extravagantly grateful words. A person who feels obliged to reciprocate a kindness in full measure, plus associated costs, finishes by rendering us in return a service which may be far more trouble to him than the original good deed was to us. Most men are too perverse to find the presence of a benefactor anything but extremely embarrassing. It seems to hurt their pride.

CHRISTOPHER: Your philosophy, sir, appears to have left you breathless. Well and good! You'll see that I'm no less magnanimous than yourself. I'll go at once. In a quarter of an hour, sir, be ready to mount!

Scene 5

The TRAVELLER and the YOUNG LADY.

TRAVELLER: I've not gone out of my way to be familiar with this man, but it certainly hasn't stopped him being familiar with me.

YOUNG LADY: Why are you leaving us, sir? Why are you standing here all alone? Are you that tired of our company after so few hours in our midst? I would feel hurt if so. I do my best to be agreeable to everybody... I'd be most unhappy to think I'd been disagreeable to you, of all people.

TRAVELLER: Forgive me, ma'am! I was just telling my servant to get everything ready for our departure.

YOUNG LADY: Departure? What are you talking about? You've barely arrived! It might well be, after staying a year, the idea of leaving might occur to you in a fit of melancholy. But not after spending less than one whole day with us! It's really too naughty of you! I must tell you frankly: you'll make me angry, if you so much as mention it again.

TRAVELLER: You couldn't threaten me with anything more painful.

YOUNG LADY: No? Are you serious? Would you be sorely wounded, if I were angry with you?

TRAVELLER: Who could be indifferent to the anger of a charming young lady?

YOUNG LADY: You sound a little as though you're joking. But I mean to take you seriously, even if I'm mistaken. Very well, sir. I may have some slight charm, as I've been told, but I assure you once more that I will be most terribly – frightfully – furious if you refer again to your departure between now and the New Year!

TRAVELLER: Most kind of you to set so generous a time limit. But would you turn me out of doors in mid-winter and the most inclement weather – ?

YOUNG LADY: Who said anything of the sort? All I mean is that around that time, you might – for form's sake – begin thinking about the date of your departure. Even so, we wouldn't let you go; we'd beg you –

TRAVELLER: Perhaps also for form's sake?

YOUNG LADY: Oh come, sir! One wouldn't have thought so honest a face could also make mock. Ah, here comes Papa! I must fly! Don't let him know I was here with you! He's always telling me off for being too fond of male company.

Scene 6

The BARON and the TRAVELLER.

BARON: Wasn't my daughter with you just now? Why did the little rascal run away?

TRAVELLER: What a priceless boon it must be to have a daughter so charming and so light-hearted! Her discourse is utterly enchanting; such gentle innocence and unaffected wit!

BARON: You are too generous in your opinion of her. She rarely mixes with girls of her own sort and possesses only to a minor degree the art of pleasing – not easy to learn in the country, though it's often more attractive than beauty itself. In her, nature has been left to its own devices, so to speak.

TRAVELLER: Which is all the more captivating because it's so rarely the case in cities. There, everything is distorted, forced and studied. Yes, things have got to the point where the words stupidity, vulgarity and nature are treated as synonymous.

BARON: Could anything give me greater pleasure than to find how completely our thoughts and judgements coincide? Oh, why couldn't I have found a friend like you ages ago?

TRAVELLER: Are you not being unfair to your other friends?

BARON: Other friends? I'm fifty years old; acquaintances I've had, but never a friend as yet. Nor did friendship ever appear to me so appealing as during these last few hours in which I've striven to win your own. What must I do to deserve it?

TRAVELLER: My friendship counts for so little that the mere desire to possess it is sufficient reason to receive it. Your request itself is worth far more than what you request.

BARON: Oh, but my dear sir, the friendship of a benefactor –

TRAVELLER: Forgive me – is not real friendship. If you view me in this false light, I really cannot be your friend.

Suppose for a moment that I were your benefactor, should I not then be obliged to fear that your friendship was really no more, in effect, than gratitude?

BARON: Cannot both be happily combined?

TRAVELLER: Very difficult! Gratitude is seen by a person of noble disposition as a duty; friendship, however, calls for a spontaneous inclination of the soul.

BARON: But how am I supposed to – ? I'm bewildered by your fastidious distinction between the two.

TRAVELLER: Pray don't esteem me more highly than I deserve! At best, I'm simply a man who was happy to do his duty. But duty in itself merits no gratitude. Moreover, since doing my duty was a pleasure, your friendship alone is for me sufficient reward.

BARON: I am more than ever confused by such magnanimity. But perhaps I am being impertinent. So far I have not made bold to inquire your name and professional status. It could be that I am offering my friendship to one who might have – er – reason to despise it –

TRAVELLER: Forgive me, sir! But you're really – I mean your thoughts exaggerate my importance.

BARON: (*Aside.*) Should I ask him? He might take my curiosity amiss.

TRAVELLER: (*Aside.*) What shall I say if he asks me?

BARON: (*Aside.*) If I don't ask him, he may think it boorish of me.

TRAVELLER: (*Aside.*) Shall I tell him the truth?

BARON: (*Aside.*) Better play safe. I'll first question his servant.

TRAVELLER: (*Aside.*) I wish I could be spared these complications!

BARON: Why so pensive?

TRAVELLER: I was about to ask you the same question, sir.

BARON: I know, one forgets oneself every so often. Let's talk about something else. Do you think the people who attacked me were, in fact, Jews? I've just been told by my village headman that he met three of them on the highroad a few days ago. By his description, they looked more like scoundrels than honest folk. And why should I doubt it?

People so intent on making profits are not going to worry overmuch about how they do it – fairly or not, by cunning or violence. They do seem to be cut out for commerce – or, not to put too fine a point upon it – plain trickery. Politeness, frankness, enterprise, discretion are all qualities which would commend the Jews to our esteem, if they didn't all too frequently employ them to our disadvantage. (*Slight pause.*) Besides, the Jews have caused me not a little damage and vexation. While I was still on active service, I once allowed myself to be persuaded to act as joint signatory to a promissory note for an acquaintance of mine. But the Jew to whom it was made out, saw to it that, not only did I have to pay him once but twice, into the bargain! Oh yes, they're a vile, wicked lot! Don't you agree? You look quite overcome.

TRAVELLER: What can I say? I must admit I've very often heard that complaint –

BARON: But isn't it a fact that something about their features predisposes us against them? It's as though one could read it in their eyes: a treacherous look – a lack of conscience, a self-seeking quality, deception and perjury. But why do you turn away?

TRAVELLER: It would seem, from what you say, that you're a great connoisseur of features and I'm a little concerned lest my own –

BARON: Oh, you offend me! How could you suspect anything of the sort? Without being a connoisseur of faces, I'm bound to say that I've never come across a face more honest, magnanimous or pleasing than your own.

TRAVELLER: To tell you the truth, I'm much opposed to sweeping judgements applied to any people as a whole. I hope you won't mind my taking the liberty of saying so. I would prefer to believe that there are good and bad individuals in every nation – among the Jews as well.

Scene 7

YOUNG LADY, TRAVELLER and BARON.

YOUNG LADY: Ah! Papa –

BARON: So there you are, shy squirrel! You ran away from
me just now! What was the meaning of that?

YOUNG LADY: I wasn't running away from you, Papa; only
from your reprimand.

BARON: The difference is very subtle. But what were you
doing to merit my reprimand?

YOUNG LADY: You know very well, Papa. You saw me... I
was here with the gentleman.

BARON: Well, what of it?

YOUNG LADY: The gentleman is a male person and
you ordered me not to have too much to do with male
persons...

BARON: You should have been able to see for yourself that
this gentleman is an exception. I would be very gratified
if he found you at all tolerable. Indeed, I'd be delighted to
see you with him constantly.

YOUNG LADY: Alas! You have probably seen me with him
for the first and last time, Papa. His servant is packing their
luggage now. That's what I came to tell you.

BARON: What? Who? His servant?

TRAVELLER: A fact, sir. I've given him his orders.
My private arrangements and fear of causing you
inconvenience make it –

BARON: What am I to think for ever after? Am I to be
denied the pleasure of demonstrating more clearly that
you have won the devotion of a grateful heart? Pray,
add to the favour you have done me in saving my life, a
second bounty no less precious: stay with me a little longer
– at least a few days. I would reproach myself for ever, if
I allowed such a man as yourself to depart – unknown,
unhonoured, unrewarded – when I had the means to do
otherwise. I have already invited some of my relatives here
today to share with them my delight and the pleasure of
becoming acquainted with my guardian angel.

TRAVELLER: My dear sir, I fear I am obliged –
YOUNG LADY: Stay with us, sir! You must stay! Please! I'll
run and tell your servant he's to unpack again. But here he
comes!

Scene 8

*Enter CHRISTOPHER, booted and spurred, carrying a saddle
bag under each arm. Other characters as before.*

CHRISTOPHER: There we are, sir! All packed and ready.
Let's be on our way. I should cut short your goodbyes. No
point in making long speeches, since we're not able to stay.
BARON: What's preventing you, then?
CHRISTOPHER: Certain considerations, Baron,
deriving from the stubbornness of my master, using his
magnanimity as an excuse.
TRAVELLER: My servant frequently talks out of turn. Please
forgive him. I can see that your pleas are, in fact, more
than mere compliments. So I surrender – for fear that
– in my eagerness to avoid appearing churlish – I should
nevertheless behave in a churlish manner.
BARON: Oh, I'm so grateful to you!
TRAVELLER: You may go and unpack once more. We'll be
staying till tomorrow.
YOUNG LADY: (*To CHRISTOPHER.*) Well? Didn't you hear?
What are you waiting for? Off you go and unpack!
CHRISTOPHER: I've every right to be angry. I can almost
feel my fury mounting...but since there's nothing worse in
store this time than staying here to eat and drink and be
well looked after, so be it! At the same time, I don't like
being made to do unnecessary jobs. Is that clear?
TRAVELLER: Hold your tongue! You're being insolent!
CHRISTOPHER: I'm just speaking the truth.
YOUNG LADY: Oh, how splendid that you'll be staying on!
Now I can be nice to you again. Come, I want to show you
our garden. You'll like it.
TRAVELLER: If you like it, ma'am, it's good as certain I
shall.

YOUNG LADY: Come along then…it'll soon be time to eat. You've no objection, Papa?

BARON: Why, no! I'll even accompany you.

YOUNG LADY: Oh, no, Papa, we wouldn't dream of imposing on you. You must have things to do.

BARON: Nothing is more important to me at present than the pleasure of my guest.

YOUNG LADY: He won't hold it against you – will you, sir? (*Softly to the TRAVELLER.*) Say 'no'. I wish to walk alone with you.

TRAVELLER: I shall regret having allowed myself to be so easily persuaded to stay, if I cause you the slightest embarrassment. So I pray you –

BARON: Why take any notice of what the child says?

YOUNG LADY: Child, indeed! Papa! Don't humiliate me! The gentleman will be thinking how young I am. (*To the TRAVELLER.*) Pay no attention. I'm old enough to go for a stroll with you. Do come along – ! But look, your servant is still standing there with those bags under each arm.

CHRISTOPHER: I would have thought that concerns only the injured party.

TRAVELLER: Be quiet! You're being treated with too much consideration!

Scene 9

Enter LISETTE. Others as before.

BARON: (*Seeing LISETTE approach.*) I'll follow you shortly, sir, if you'd care to accompany my daughter to the garden.

YOUNG LADY: Stay here as long as you please, Papa. We'll pass the time pleasantly enough. This way, come along! (*Exeunt YOUNG LADY and TRAVELLER.*)

BARON: Lisette, I want a word with you!

LISETTE: Sir?

BARON: (*Softly.*) I don't yet know who our guest is and, for various reasons, I don't wish to ask him directly. Do you think you could – perhaps – from his servant, eh?

LISETTE: I quite understand. My curiosity brought me this

way with that very thought in mind.

BARON: Good, see what you can learn and report to me later. I shall make it worth your while.

LISETTE: Leave it to me.

CHRISTOPHER: I'm sure you won't take it amiss, sir, if we really make ourselves at home here. But please, don't put yourself out on my account. I'm perfectly happy with things as they are.

BARON: Lisette, I'll leave you to look after him. Just see he has everything he needs. (*Exit BARON.*)

CHRISTOPHER: So, Mam'zelle, I commend myself to your kind keeping, which will ensure that I lack for nothing. (*Prepares to withdraw.*)

Scene 10

LISETTE and CHRISTOPHER.

LISETTE: (*Detaining him.*) Oh no, sir, I can't find it in my heart to let you be so discourteous! Am I then not woman enough to merit a short conversation?

CHRISTOPHER: Bless my soul! You're quick off the mark, Mam'zelle! Whether you're woman enough or too much of one, I cannot say. To judge by your ready tongue, I'd almost warrant it's the latter. But be that as it may; you'll have to excuse me. As you can see, my hands and arms are full… The moment I feel hungry or thirsty, though, I'll be with you again right away.

LISETTE: Just like our chief groom!

CHRISTOPHER: Well, I'll be damned! He must be a shrewd fellow if he takes after me!

LISETTE: He's on his chain in the courtyard, if you'd like to meet him.

CHRISTOPHER: Strike me! You must mean the dog! I see you thought I was referring to physical hunger and thirst. Not so. What I had in mind was the hunger and thirst for love. That's what I meant, Mam'zelle! There! Are you satisfied with my declaration?

LISETTE: Better than with what you've declared.

CHRISTOPHER: Look here, between ourselves: am I to take

it from what you say, that a declaration of love from me would not be unwelcome?

LISETTE: Perhaps! Do you want to make me one? Seriously?

CHRISTOPHER: Perhaps!

LISETTE: Pah! What sort of an answer is that? Perhaps!

CHRISTOPHER: Not one iota different from your own!

LISETTE: On my lips, however, the word means something else entirely. 'Perhaps' is a girl's surest safeguard. However poorly we play, we must never show our hand.

CHRISTOPHER: Yes, if game it be! I thought we were getting down to brass tacks. (*He flings the two bags on the ground.*) Don't know why I should take so much trouble! To hell with them! I love you, Mam'zelle!

LISETTE: That's what I call saying a great deal in very few words! Let's analyse them.

CHRISTOPHER: No, no – rather let them be. But so that we can quietly share our thoughts, do sit down. Standing makes me tired. Relax! (*Invites her to sit on one of the bags.*) – I love you, Mam'zelle!

LISETTE: But – this is a devilish hard seat. Must be stuffed with books –

CHRISTOPHER: Yes – some of them very tender and witty, too! Yet you find them hard to sit on? That's my master's travelling library, consisting of comedies to make you weep, tragedies good for a laugh, tenderly heroic poems, profoundly thoughtful drinking-songs and the Lord knows what else besides. But let's change places. Sit on my bag if you like. Don't stand on ceremony! Mine's softer.

LISETTE: Forgive me! I won't be as rude as all that!

CHRISTOPHER: Don't fuss! Do as you like – no compliments needed! You'd sooner not? Then, I'll carry you across.

LISETTE: Since you're ordering me – (*She stands up and moves to sit on the other bag.*)

CHRISTOPHER: Ordering? God forbid! No, not ordering – that would be going too far. But if that's how it strikes you, best stay where you are! (*He sits down again on his own bag.*)

LISETTE: (*Aside.*) What a clod-hopper! But I'll just have to put up with it –

CHRISTOPHER: Where had we got to? Oh, yes – love. The thing is I love you, Mam'zelle. *Je vous aime*, as I'd say, if you were a French marquise.

LISETTE: For heaven's sake! You're a Frenchman, then?

CHRISTOPHER: No… I'm ashamed to confess, I'm only a German. But I've been lucky enough to be able to mix with various Frenchmen and that's how I've learned, more or less, how a well-bred fellow behaves. You need only look at me.

LISETTE: Perhaps you and your master have just come from France?

CHRISTOPHER: Oh, no!

LISETTE: Where else, then? Somewhere, presumably?

CHRISTOPHER: A few miles – er – behind France. That's where we came from.

LISETTE: Could it have been Italy?

CHRISTOPHER: Not far off.

LISETTE: England, then?

CHRISTOPHER: Almost right. England is one of its provinces. We're a good fifty miles from home. But, Lord bless us and save us, my horses! The poor beasts are still saddled. Forgive me, Mam'zelle – quick! Up you get! (*Picks up the bags, replacing them under each arm.*) Notwithstanding the fervour of my love, I must first go and do the necessary. We've still got all day and – more to the point – all night – ahead of us. We'll see eye to eye before we've done… I expect I'll be able to find you again.

Scene 11

MARTIN CROOK and LISETTE.

LISETTE: I'll not get much out of him. Too stupid or too wily. Either way, unfathomable!

CROOK: Well, Miss Lisette? Has that fellow been trying to cut me out?

LISETTE: He had no need to.

CROOK: No need? And there was I thinking my place in

your heart was secure against all comers!

LISETTE: That's what you may have thought, sir. Your sort are entitled to their absurd fancies... Nor does it bother me what you may have thought. But that you should say it, is quite another matter. What has my heart got to do with you, I'd like to know! What favours, what presents of yours have earned you any such right? Hearts these days aren't just given away like that, you know! Why should you think I'm all that keen to dispose of mine? I'll make sure I find myself a decent, reliable man before I cast my pearl.

CROOK: Devil take it! Looks like I'm catching a cold here for my pains! A pinch of snuff might do the trick... See if I can't sneeze it away! (*He takes out the stolen snuff box, plays about with it for a moment or two and finally, in laughably arrogant fashion, inhales a pinch of tobacco.*)

LISETTE: (*With a sidelong glance at him.*) Heavens, where on earth did the fellow come by that snuff box?

CROOK: Care for a pinch?

LISETTE: Oh, master Bailiff, sir! I'm your most obedient servant! (*She takes a pinch.*)

CROOK: Nothing like a silver snuff box for reaching the heart. An earwig couldn't slip in more adroitly!

LISETTE: Is the box real silver?

CROOK: Would Martin Crook possess it, if not?

LISETTE: May I take a closer look?

CROOK: Yes, but only if I hold it.

LISETTE: The design is outstanding!

CROOK: Must weigh all of four ounces...

LISETTE: I'd love to have a box like that, for the sake of the design alone.

CROOK: If ever I have it melted down, the design will be at your disposal.

LISETTE: You're too generous! A present, no doubt?

CROOK: Yes – didn't cost me a cent.

LISETTE: I warrant any woman would be swept off her feet by a present like that. It could secure your happiness, Master Bailiff. For my part, I'd be hard put to defend myself, if somebody attacked me with a silver snuff box. My defeat at the hands of a lover with a box like that would be a foregone conclusion.

CROOK: I take your meaning.

LISETTE: Since it cost you nothing, Master Bailiff, take my
advice and use it to get yourself a nice lady-friend –

CROOK: I understand you – yes, indeed!

LISETTE: (*Wheedling.*) Would you be thinking of making me a
present of it, Master Bailiff?

CROOK: Beg pardon, but these days, one doesn't give away
silver boxes just like that. What makes you think I'm so
keen to dispose of mine? I'll make sure I find a decent,
reliable man before I cast my pearl, eh?

LISETTE: Did anyone ever hear such a stupidly boorish
remark? To suggest that a snuff box and a girl's heart are of
equal value!

CROOK: Why not? A heart of stone for a snuff box of silver?

LISETTE: Perhaps the heart would stop being stony if – but
what's the point of my talking? You're not worthy of my
love – what a soft-hearted silly goose I am! (*Starts to weep.*)
I'd almost begun to believe the estate manager was one of
those trustworthy men who mean what they say –

CROOK: And what a soft-hearted idiot I've been to think a
woman ever means what she says! There, Lisette my dear,
don't cry! (*He gives her the box.*) Now, am I worthy of your
love? And to start with, I desire nothing more than to give
your beautiful hand a little kiss! (*Does so.*) Ah, that tastes so
good!

Scene 12

YOUNG LADY, LISETTE and MARTIN CROOK.

YOUNG LADY: (*Creeps up on him and presses his head to her
hand.*) Come Master Bailiff, won't you kiss my hand as
well?

LISETTE: Whatever next!

CROOK: Most willingly, ma'am! (*Goes to kiss her hand.*)

YOUNG LADY: (*Slaps his face.*) Stupid! Don't you know when
something's meant as a joke?

CROOK: A devilish poor joke, if you ask me!

LISETTE: (*Laughing at him.*) Oh, I'm sorry for you, my dear
Bailiff – ha, ha, ha!

CROOK: You are? And all you can do is laugh at me! Is that
the thanks I get? Very well. We shall see!
(*Exit CROOK.*)

LISETTE: (*Continues laughing.*) Ha, ha!

Scene 13

LISETTE and YOUNG LADY.

YOUNG LADY: I'd never have believed it, if I hadn't seen it
myself. Getting yourself kissed! And by the Bailiff at that!

LISETTE: I don't know what right you've got to eavesdrop on
me. I thought you went for a stroll in the garden with that
stranger.

YOUNG LADY: Yes, and I'd still be with him if Papa hadn't
come after us. I wasn't able to have a sensible talk with
him. Papa is so straitlaced –

LISETTE: What do you mean by 'sensible'? What did you
want to discuss, that wasn't fit for your Papa to hear?

YOUNG LADY: No end of things! But you'll make me angry,
if you go on quizzing me! If you must know, I've rather
taken a fancy to the strange gentleman. I suppose I may
confess that much!

LISETTE: I suppose you'd have a fearful row with your
Papa, if he tried to marry you off to a husband like that?
Seriously though, who knows what's in his mind? It's only
a pity you're not a year or two older, or it might just come
about.

YOUNG LADY: If it were only a matter of age, Papa could
easily make me out to be a couple of years older. I
certainly wouldn't contradict him.

LISETTE: No! I've got a better idea. I'll give you a few of *my*
years. That will help us both. *I* won't be too old and *you'll*
not be too young.

YOUNG LADY: True enough! What a splendid notion!

LISETTE: I must have a word with the stranger's servant.
He's just coming. It'll be to your advantage. Just leave me

alone with him. Off you go –

YOUNG LADY: You won't forget what you said about our ages, will   you? Remember, Lisette!

Scene 14

LISETTE and CHRISTOPHER.

LISETTE: You must be either hungry or thirsty, sir – coming back so soon, I mean.

CHRISTOPHER: Indeed I am – but you haven't forgotten what I explained about my hunger and thirst? To tell you the truth, dear lady, they came over me the moment I first set eyes on you, as I was dismounting here yesterday. But believing that we'd be staying only a couple of hours, I thought it was hardly worth while getting to know you. We couldn't have got very far with so little time. We'd have had to start our romance from the end and work backwards. Only thing is, one can never be quite sure of pulling a cat out of the stove by its tail.

LISETTE: Very true! However, we can now tackle things in the proper order. You can make your proposal. I can reply. I'll voice my doubts. You can resolve them for me. We can each think carefully in advance about every step we take. That way, nobody'll be sold a pig in a poke. Had you proposed to me yesterday, there and then, it's true I'd have accepted. But just think what a risk I would have been taking, with no time to find out about your status or means, country of origin, residence and all the rest of it.

CHRISTOPHER: I'll be damned! Would you have needed to know all that? You could hardly have made more fuss, if we were getting married!

LISETTE: Oh, if it were merely marriage we had in view, I'd have been silly to be so finicky. A love affair is a different thing entirely! The merest trifle becomes a matter of major importance. So don't count on receiving the least token of my favour, unless you can first satisfy my curiosity in every particular.

CHRISTOPHER: Is that so? Well, how far does your curiosity extend?

LISETTE: Since a servant can always best be judged according to his master, I'd first like to know –

CHRISTOPHER: – Who my master is? Ha, ha! Funnily enough, that's a question I'd gladly put to yourself, if I thought you might know any more than I do.

LISETTE: Don't think you can get away with a threadbare excuse like that! In short, I must know who your master is, or that's the end of our friendship, here and now!

CHRISTOPHER: I've only known my master barely four weeks. That was when he took me into his service in Hamburg. I've accompanied him ever since, without once troubling to inquire his name or status. One thing is certain: he's rich. For neither he nor I have wanted for anything during our travels. What more do I need to worry about?

LISETTE: How could I count on your love, if you refuse to entrust even such a trifle to my discretion? I would never behave like that to you. For example, I have here a beautiful silver snuff box –

CHRISTOPHER: Yes? What about it?

LISETTE: You need only ask me nicely and I'll tell you who gave it to me –

CHRISTOPHER: I'm not all that interested, really. I'd sooner know whom *you* intend to give it to.

LISETTE: I've not yet made up my mind on that score. But if it doesn't come your way, you'll have nobody but yourself to blame... I would certainly not fail to reward frankness on your part.

CHRISTOPHER: Frankness? A wagging tongue, more like it! But, sure as I'm an honest fellow, if I'm silent on certain matters, it's of necessity. I really don't know what I could gossip about. Damn it! I'd be delighted to spill all my secrets – if only I had a few!

LISETTE: Goodbye, then! I shall no longer lay siege to your virtue. I only hope it may soon win you a silver snuff box and a sweetheart like those it has just deprived you of. (*About to leave.*)

CHRISTOPHER: Where are you off to? Easy does it! (*Aside.*) I've no choice but to lie. All said and done, can I afford to lose a present like that? Anyway, what harm can it do?

LISETTE: Are you going to give me some details? But, no – I can see it's too much for you. No, no! I don't want to know anything –

CHRISTOPHER: Yes, yes – you shall know all! (*Aside.*) If only I were a practised liar! (*Aloud.*) Listen! My master is – of noble blood. He comes – that is – we've come together from – from – Holland. He was obliged to flee – because of certain – vexations – a peccadillo – a murder, in fact.

LISETTE: What's that you say? A murder?!

CHRISTOPHER: Yes – but a respectable murder – had to escape because of a duel – and he's now – er – on the run –

LISETTE: And you, my friend?

CHRISTOPHER: I'm on the run with him. The dead man was – I mean – the dead man's friends – had us closely pursued and because of this – er – pursuit – well, you can easily guess the rest. Damn it! What else could we have done? Consider the situation! Some brash young pup insults us. My master puts paid to him. No other way! If anyone insulted me, I'd do the same – or – or box his ears. A man of honour can't just let people walk all over him!

LISETTE: Bravo! I like that kind of man. I myself am not a one to take things lying down. But look – there's your master coming now. Who'd ever think, to look at him that he could be so furious and ferocious!

CHRISTOPHER: Come, let's keep out of his way. He may guess from my expression that I've betrayed him.

LISETTE: Well, I'm now satisfied –

CHRISTOPHER: So what about the snuff box?

LISETTE: Come with me! (*Aside.*) I'll first see how much my master thinks the secret I've discovered is worth. If he rewards me well for my pains, this fellow can have the snuff box.

Scene 15

The TRAVELLER.

TRAVELLER: I'm missing my snuff box. True, it's a trifle

but still the loss is painful. Could it have been the estate manager? Of course, I could simply have lost it. Might have pulled it out of my pocket carelessly. It's not fair to insult a person with one's suspicions. All the same, he did press up against me, reaching for my watch. I caught him in the act. Might he not also have reached for my snuff box, without my catching him?

Scene 16

MARTIN CROOK and the TRAVELLER.

CROOK: (*Catching sight of the TRAVELLER, he tries to turn back.*) Fah!

TRAVELLER: Come closer, friend! (*Aside.*) He's as nervous as if he could read my thoughts! (*Aloud.*) Hey, there! Come here a moment!

CROOK: (*Insolent.*) I haven't time. I know you want to gossip but I've more important things to do. I've no wish to hear the tale of your heroic exploits for the tenth time. Go and tell it to somebody who's not yet heard it!

TRAVELLER: Can't believe my ears! First time we met, the bailiff was forthcoming and polite; now he's downright churlish. Two-faced! Which of your masks is genuine?

CROOK: What the devil do you mean, insulting me by calling my face a mask? I don't wish to quarrel with you – otherwise – (*On the point of moving away.*)

TRAVELLER: (*Aside.*) His shameless behaviour strengthens my suspicion – but, no – I must be patient. (*Aloud.*) Look, I've something important to ask you –

CROOK: I won't answer, no matter how important it is. So you might as well save your question.

TRAVELLER: (*Aside.*) I'll risk it. But I'd be very sorry to do him an injustice. (*Aloud.*) My friend, have you by chance seen my snuff box? I'm missing it.

CROOK: What sort of a question is that? Can I help it, if somebody's stolen it from you? What do you take me for – a fence, or the thief himself?

TRAVELLER: Who said anything about stealing? You almost give yourself away –

CROOK: (*Raising his voice.*) Give myself away? So you think I
have it, eh? Do you know what it means to accuse an
honest man of something like that? Have you any idea?

TRAVELLER: What are you shouting for? I haven't accused
you of anything so far. You accuse yourself! Come to that, I
don't know that I *would* be doing you an injustice, if I did.
Who was it I caught, a short while ago, trying to snatch my
watch?

CROOK: I see you're the sort who can't take a joke. Look
here – (*Aside.*) I hope he didn't see the box with Lisette!
– She surely couldn't have been such a fool as to start
boasting about it –

TRAVELLER: So well can I take a joke that I'm prepared to
believe you were just having a bit of fun with my snuff
box. But carry a joke too far, and it finally turns into
something serious. I am concerned for your good name.
Even if I were convinced you meant no harm, others might
take a different view –

CROOK: Others, you say! Others! Believe me, others would
have lost their temper long since, being blamed for a thing
like that. But if you think I've got it, you're welcome to feel
my pockets. Go on, search me!

TRAVELLER: That's not my business. Besides, a man doesn't
carry everything about in his pocket.

CROOK: All right! Just to let you see I'm an honest fellow,
I'll turn out my own pockets. Here, take a look! (*Aside.*) It
would have to be the work of the devil for that box to fall
out!

TRAVELLER Don't bother!

CROOK: No, no! I want to show you! See for yourself! (*He
turns out one pocket.*) Any sign of a snuff box there? Nothing
but breadcrumbs! Precious possessions! (*He turns out the
other.*) Nothing here either! Ah, yes – one small calendar.
I keep it for the sake of the verses each month. They're a
real laugh! Never mind, let's get on with it! There you are
– look! I'm turning the third pocket inside out! (*As he does
so, two large beards come to light.*) Devil take me! What's that
I dropped?

(*He darts to snatch them up, but the TRAVELLER is
quicker and manages to seize one of the beards.*)

TRAVELLER: What have we here?

CROOK: (*Aside.*) Damn and blast! I thought I'd already got rid of that rubbish!

TRAVELLER: This is a beard, isn't it? (*He holds it up to his chin.*) Doesn't it make me look just like a Jew?

CROOK: Give that to me! Here, hand it over! Who knows what you'll be thinking next! I use it to scare my little boy now and again. That's what it's for.

TRAVELLER: Be good enough to leave it with me. I'd quite like to give somebody a fright myself.

CROOK: Don't you try playing any tricks with me! I must have it back. (*He tries to snatch it from his hand but fails.*)

TRAVELLER: Be off with you, or –

CROOK: (*Aside.*) Blast him! How the devil am I going to get out of this one? (*Aloud.*) Very well, no matter! I see you're set on making trouble for me. But, devil take me if I'm not an honest man! You'll not find a soul to say a word against me. Just you bear that in mind! Whatever happens, I can swear on oath, I've never used that beard for any wicked purpose! (*Exit BAILIFF.*)

Scene 17

The TRAVELLER.

TRAVELLER: The fellow himself has aroused suspicions in my mind, much to his disadvantage. Could he have been one of those robbers in disguise? However, I must be careful not to jump to conclusions.

Scene 18

The BARON and the TRAVELLER.

TRAVELLER: Wouldn't you think I'd ripped the beard from the face of one of those Jewish highwaymen during yesterday's struggle? (*Shows him the beard.*)

BARON: I don't quite follow you, sir. But why did you abandon me so abruptly in the garden?

TRAVELLER: Forgive my discourtesy! I meant to return at once. I only went to look for my snuff box, thinking I must have lost it hereabouts.

BARON: I'm extremely sorry to hear it. I hate to think of your suffering further damage on my account!

TRAVELLER: The damage would not be all that great. But do take a closer look at this handsome beard!

BARON: You've already shown it to me. What about it?

TRAVELLER: Let me explain myself more clearly. I believe – but no – I'd better keep my suspicions to myself.

BARON: Suspicions? Do please explain!

TRAVELLER: No. I spoke too hastily. I could be mistaken.

BARON: You disturb me.

TRAVELLER: What do you think of the bailiff – your estate manager?

BARON: No, no. Don't try to change the subject! I entreat you, by the kindness you've already shown me, tell me what it is that you believe or suspect. How might you be mistaken?

TRAVELLER: Only by answering my question could you induce me to tell you.

BARON: What do I think of my bailiff? Why, I consider him to be a thoroughly reliable and trustworthy man.

TRAVELLER: Then please forget I was about to say something.

BARON: A beard – suspicions – my bailiff? I fail to see the connection. Won't you be moved by my pleas and explain yourself? You said you might be mistaken? Let's suppose you were: what danger could threaten you in a friend's house?

TRAVELLER: You press me too hard! I'll tell you what's on my mind. Your bailiff inadvertently dropped this beard. A second one which fell, he managed to retrieve at great speed. Moreover, from what he had to say for himself, I got the impression of a man who believes people think him quite capable of the misdeeds which, in fact, he commits. Finally, I caught him making a none too serious or, at least, none too skilful attempt to pick my pocket.

BARON: It's as though my eyes were suddenly opened. I'll

look into this right away. I suspect you are not mistaken.
And you really had qualms about bringing such a grave
matter to my attention? I'll go at once and do all in my
power to get at the truth. Can it be that my would-be
murderer is here in my own household?

TRAVELLER: But don't be angry with me if you discover
that, fortunately, my suspicions are unfounded. You
dragged them out of me, otherwise I would certainly have
kept quiet.

BARON: Whether or not your suspicions turn out to be
justified, I shall always be grateful to you for confiding in
me.

Scene 19

The TRAVELLER; later CHRISTOPHER.

TRAVELLER: I only hope he won't deal with him too hastily.
Great as my suspicions may be, the man could still be
innocent. I'm in a quandary. It's no trifling matter to arouse
a master's distrust of his employees. Even if he finds them
innocent, he will have lost faith in them for ever. The more
I think about it, the more I feel I should not have spoken.
Aren't people going to say my suspicions were prompted
by self-interest or desire for revenge when they hear how
I blamed the bailiff for the loss of my snuff box? I'd give a
lot to be able to halt this investigation, if only I could –

CHRISTOPHER: (*Arrives laughing.*) Ha, ha! Do you know
who you are, sir?

TRAVELLER: Do you know what a fool *you* are? Why ask
such a question?

CHRISTOPHER: Very well. If you don't know, I'll tell you.
You're of noble birth. You've just arrived from Holland
where you ran into problems and fought a duel in which
you had the good fortune to stab some brash young
jackanapes. Hotly pursued by the dead man's friends, you
were forced to flee the country and I, sir, have had the
honour of accompanying you in your flight.

TRAVELLER: Are you dreaming, or have you gone mad?

CHRISTOPHER: Neither. The story's too clever for a
madman, too crazy for a dreamer.

TRAVELLER: Who's been having you on with such
ridiculous nonsense?

CHRISTOPHER: That'll be the day, when somebody can
fool me! Don't you agree it's a well-concocted yarn?
I didn't have much time to invent my lies, but even so,
I could hardly have cooked up anything better. At least
you're now proof against further curiosity!

TRAVELLER: But what am I supposed to make of all that?

CHRISTOPHER: Only what pleases you. Leave the rest to
me. I'll tell you how it all came about. I was questioned
about your name, status, country of birth, business and
so on. Nor was it long before I told all I knew – that is
to say, nothing! As you can imagine, my answer was
deemed inadequate and gave my questioner no cause for
satisfaction. I was pressed further – but in vain. Having
nothing to say, I said nothing. Finally, I was offered a
present which induced me to tell more than I knew – that
is to say, I lied.

TRAVELLER: You scoundrel! I can see I'm in really good
hands, with you for a servant.

CHRISTOPHER: You don't mean to say I came more or less
close to lying the truth?

TRAVELLER: You shameless prevaricator! You've placed me
in an embarrassing situation from which –

CHRISTOPHER: – From which you can easily escape by
spreading the knowledge of that flattering epithet you've
just conferred upon me – liar, to wit!

TRAVELLER: But by the same token, wouldn't I then be
obliged to reveal who I am?

CHRISTOPHER: So much the better! That would also
give *me* a chance to get to know you. It's for you to
judge whether, in good conscience, I should have a bad
conscience for having lied. (*He pulls out the snuff box.*) Just
look at this box! Could I have earned it more easily?

TRAVELLER: Let me see it! (*Takes hold of it.*) What's this?

CHRISTOPHER: (*Laughing.*) I thought you'd be astonished!
Tell me, wouldn't you yourself have played a few tricks

with the truth for the sake of a box like that, eh?

TRAVELLER: Then it was you who stole it from me?

CHRISTOPHER: What, me? How?

TRAVELLER: It isn't your breach of trust that troubles me so much as the fact that my over-hasty suspicions fell on an honest man. And you still have the crass impudence to try to persuade me that this was a present – no less disgracefully obtained? Be off with you! And don't let me ever set eyes on you again!

CHRISTOPHER: Are you dreaming, or – ? Respect forbids me to suggest the alternative. Surely, it can't be jealousy that leads you to indulge in such fantasies? This box, you say, is yours – and I'm supposed – forgive the expression – to have stolen it from you? If that were so, would I be such a nincompoop as to boast about it to your face? – Ah, that's good! Here's Lisette! Quick, come over here and help me put my master to rights!

Scene 20

LISETTE, TRAVELLER and CHRISTOPHER.

LISETTE: Oh, sir, what a lot of botheration you're causing us all! What did our bailiff do to harm you? The master's furious with him because of you. There's talk of beards, boxes and plunder! The bailiff is in tears, swearing that he's innocent and you're telling untruths. There's no calming the master. He's even sent for the village headman and the magistrates to have him locked up. What's the meaning of all this?

CHRISTOPHER: That's not the half of it! Just you listen to what he's been saying about me –

TRAVELLER: Yes, indeed, my dear Lisette – I was too hasty. The bailiff is innocent. This godless servant of mine has landed me in all these vexations. It's he who stole my snuff box, causing me to suspect the bailiff. The beard may well have been what the bailiff said it was – a play-thing to scare the children. I'll go now and offer him compensation, admit I was mistaken. Anything he wants, I'll give him.

CHRISTOPHER: No, no – hold hard! First, you must

compensate me! For heaven's sake, Lisette, speak up and tell him the truth of the matter. Be hanged to you and your wretched snuff box! Am I to let myself be branded a thief on your account? Didn't you give me the snuff box as a present?

LISETTE: Of course I did. And you shall keep it.

TRAVELLER: So that much is true, is it? But the snuff box belongs to me!

LISETTE: To you? That I did not know!

TRAVELLER: So it was Lisette who found it? And my carelessness is to blame for all this confusion? (*To CHRISTOPHER.*) I've done you a great wrong as well! Forgive me! I'm thoroughly ashamed of myself for acting so hastily!

LISETTE: (*Aside.*) God in heaven! I'm beginning to see through it all! He didn't act too hastily!

TRAVELLER: Come along, let's –

Scene 21

BARON, TRAVELLER, LISETTE and CHRISTOPHER.

BARON: (*Quickly joining them.*) Lisette, return the gentleman's snuff box to him this instant! Everything's now quite clear. The bailiff's made a full confession. Weren't you ashamed to accept a present from a man like that? Now then, where's the box?

TRAVELLER: So it's true, after all!

LISETTE: The gentleman already has it. Since you were accepting the bailiff's services, I saw no harm in accepting a present from him. It seems I knew him no better than you did.

CHRISTOPHER: So much for my present, blast it! Easy come, easy go!

BARON: But how can I express my gratitude to you, dear friend? A second time you've saved me from a danger no less great than the first. I owe you my life. Without you, I'd never have discovered my imminent peril in time. It turns out that his villainous accomplice was the village headman

whom I believed to be the most trustworthy individual on
my whole estate. How would I ever have guessed it! Had
you left us today as you planned –

TRAVELLER: – True, the assistance I thought to have
rendered you yesterday would have remained far from
complete. I count myself fortunate indeed to have been
selected by Providence as the agent of this unsuspected
revelation... I am now trembling as much with delight, as I
was previously, for fear of being mistaken.

BARON: I admire your philanthropy as I do your
magnanimity. I only hope that what Lisette has told me
about you will turn out to be true!

Scene 22

YOUNG LADY and others as before.

LISETTE: And why should it not?

BARON: Come, daughter, come! Combine your plea with
mine and entreat my saviour to accept your hand and with
it my property. What could my gratitude offer him more
precious than yourself – you, whom I love as much as I
love him? (*To the TRAVELLER.*) Don't be surprised that
I should make you such a proposal – your servant has
told us who you are. Grant me the inestimable pleasure of
expressing my recognition! My means and social status are
comparable with your own. Here, you are safe from your
enemies and among friends who revere you. But you seem
dismayed! What am I to think?

YOUNG LADY: Are you worried about me? Let me assure
you I shall be only too happy to obey my father.

TRAVELLER: (*To the BARON.*) Your generosity astounds
me. Only now, measured against the immensity of the
recompense you offer me, do I fully appreciate how small
was the service I did you. But how am I to respond? My
servant did not tell you the truth and I –

BARON: Then, heaven grant that you are not what he
claimed! May your situation and fortune prove inferior to
my own! In which case, my recompense would seem all

the more precious and yourself perhaps less reluctant to grant my request.

TRAVELLER: (*Aside.*) Why should I not reveal my identity? (*Aloud.*) Sir, my soul is overwhelmed by the nobility of your spirit. I can only beg you to blame fate rather than myself, if your entreaty cannot but prove in vain. I am –

BARON: – Perhaps already married?

TRAVELLER: No –

BARON: Well, what then?

TRAVELLER: I am a Jew.

BARON: A Jew! Oh, cruel mischance!

CHRISTOPHER: A Jew?

LISETTE: A Jew?

YOUNG LADY: What of it?

LISETTE: Hush, miss! I'll tell you later!

BARON: Are there then cases in which heaven itself prevents man from being grateful?

TRAVELLER: You have no need to be.

BARON: I wish to do as much as fate will allow me. At least, take all my property! I would sooner be poor and grateful, than rich and thankless.

TRAVELLER: That offer, too, I fear, is pointless in my case. The God of my fathers has given me more than enough for my needs. In full recompense, if you will, I ask only that, in future, you should be milder and less sweeping in your judgment of my race. The reason I concealed my identity from you was not that I am ashamed of my religion. No! It was because I perceived that, while well-disposed towards me, you were averse to my nation. For my part, I have always considered the friendship of a fellow-human, whoever he may be, precious beyond measure.

BARON: I am ashamed of my behaviour.

CHRISTOPHER: I've only just recovered from my astonishment and come to my senses. What's this? You, a Jew, had the gall to take an honest Christian into your service? You should have been serving *me!* That's as the Bible would have it! Heaven help us! In my person, you insulted the whole of Christendom! That explains not only why my master would never eat pork on our travels but also countless other farcical whims. Don't imagine I'm going to accompany you any longer! On the contrary, I'll take you to court for what you did to me!

TRAVELLER: I can't expect you to think more highly of us than do the common run of Christians. I'll refrain from reminding you of the appalling conditions in Hamburg from which I rescued you. Nor do I wish to compel you to stay with me. However, since I've been reasonably satisfied with your services and because, moreover, I suspected you unjustly, I ask you to accept as compensation the object which was the cause of my suspicions. (*Gives him the snuff box.*) You will also receive your wages. Then, go wherever you wish!

CHRISTOPHER: No! I'll be damned! It seems, after all, that there are Jews who are not Jews. You are a fine man! It's a deal! I'll stay with you! A Christian would have given me a kick in the behind – rather than a snuff box!

BARON: (*To TRAVELLER.*) The more I see of you, the more you delight me. Come with me, and we'll see that the guilty parties are put under lock and key. How worthy of respect Jews would be, if only they were all like you!

TRAVELLER: And how lovable Christians would be, if only they all possessed your qualities!

(*Exeunt BARON, YOUNG LADY and TRAVELLER.*)

Scene 23

LISETTE and CHRISTOPHER.

LISETTE: So, my friend – you lied to me?

CHRISTOPHER: Yes – and for two reasons. Firstly, I didn't know the truth. Secondly, a man doesn't tell much of the truth in exchange for a snuff box he has to hand back.

LISETTE: Come to that, how do I know you, yourself, are not a Jew, however much you try to disguise it?

CHRISTOPHER: For a lady's maid, you're a sight too inquisitive! Just you come with me!

(*He gives her is arm and they walk off together.*)

The End.

NATHAN THE WISE

a dramatic poem in five acts

Characters

SULTAN SALADIN

SITTAH
his sister

NATHAN
a rich Jew of Jerusalem

RECHA
his adopted daughter

DAYA
a Christian woman living in the Jew's house
as companion to Recha

A Young TEMPLAR KNIGHT

Dervish AL HAFI

The PATRIARCH of Jerusalem

A LAY-BROTHER

An EMIR

Assorted MAMELUKES of Saladin

The action takes place in Jerusalem.

ACT ONE

Scene 1

The hall of Nathan's house.

NATHAN, on his return from a journey, is greeted by DAYA.

DAYA: Nathan himself! Well, I'll be blest! You're back! Eternal
    thanks to God, you're home at last!
NATHAN: Yes, Daya, thank the Lord! But why 'at last'?
    Would I have wished it sooner, if indeed,
    That had been possible? From Babylon –
    The way I had to come – a zigzag route –
    Home to Jerusalem's two hundred miles.
    And debt-collecting as I went, I'd have
    You know, is neither child's play, nor a task
    One can afford to skimp at will.
DAYA: Oh, Nathan,
    Here meanwhile, what desolation might
    Have been in store for you! Your house...
NATHAN: ...
    Caught fire.
    That much I heard already and, God grant,
    There's nothing more alarming left to hear.
DAYA: Burnt to the ground it could have been – your house!
NATHAN: And had it been, then we'd have built another –
    Still more comfortable.
DAYA: That may be!
    But Recha, too, was in an ace of being
    Burned.
NATHAN: What, burned alive? My darling Recha?
    That, I didn't hear. But had she been –
    Oh God, I'd need no house at all! My Recha,
    Within an ace of being burned? You mean – ?
    Was she? Is she? Not dead? Come, out with it!
    Kill me, for pity's sake! The truth! Suspense

Is torture. Tell me! Yes, she's dead!

DAYA: If so,
Would you be hearing news so dire from me?

NATHAN: Why terrify me, then? O, Recha, dearest!
My darling Recha!

DAYA: Yours, you say? Why yours?

NATHAN: God forbid I ever lose the right
To call my Recha mine!

DAYA: But do you call
All that you possess – with equal right –
Your own?

NATHAN: With greatest right in Recha's case!
Nature and luck endowed me with the rest.
But Recha is the sole possession mine
By virtue's right alone.

DAYA: How dearly, Nathan,
Must I pay for all your kindness, if
Indeed, kindness it is when exercised
With such an end in view!

NATHAN: With such an end?
What end is that?

DAYA: My conscience…

NATHAN: Daya, please,
First let me tell you all about…

DAYA: I say
My conscience…

NATHAN: All about this lovely cloth
I bought for you in Babylon. So rich
In taste and texture. Why, the one I've brought
For darling Recha's hardly any finer!

DAYA: What good is that, when – as I say – my conscience
Will now no longer let itself be lulled.

NATHAN: I long to see how you will like the brooch,
The bangles, ear-rings, pendant and the chain
I got you in Damascus –

DAYA: That's your style!
All's well, provided you are giving presents!

NATHAN: Take them as gladly as I give – and hush!

DAYA: Not a word! Oh, Nathan, who could doubt
Your honour or your magnanimity?
And yet...
NATHAN: I'm just a Jew, all said and done!
That's what you mean?
DAYA: No, Nathan, what I mean
You know full well.
NATHAN: Then say no more.
DAYA: I won't.
But should offence to God thereby result –
Something I cannot change nor yet prevent –
Then be it on your head –
NATHAN: On my head be it!
Where is she then? Where is she hiding? Daya,
If you're deceiving me...! Does Recha know
I'm here, that I've arrived?
DAYA: It's hard to say!
She's trembling yet with fear, in every limb –
For ever, in her mind's eye, seeing fire.
Her soul's awake by night and sleeps by day:
Less than animal, she seems at times;
At others, more than angel.
NATHAN: My poor child!
What are we humans?
DAYA: Long she lay in bed
This morning, eyes shut, motionless – as though
She'd died. Then suddenly starts up and cries:
Hark! I hear my father's camels coming;
Even the gentle music of his voice!
Then closed her eyes once more and her poor head,
Denied her arm's support, dropped on the pillow.
I rushed outside and, sure enough, I saw
Your caravan approaching, as she said –
A miracle! The whole time, so it seems,
Her soul had been with you – and him –
NATHAN: With
whom?
Who's 'him'?
DAYA: The one who saved her from the flames,
Who else?

NATHAN: Who was it? What's his name? Where is he?
　　　Who saved my Recha for me? Who is he?
DAYA: He's a young Templar Knight who recently
　　　Was taken prisoner, transported here,
　　　Then pardoned by Sultan Saladin –
NATHAN:　　　　　　　　　　　　What's that?
　　　A Templar left alive by Saladin?
　　　My Recha owes her life to miracle
　　　So rare? Thank God!
DAYA:　　　　　　Had he not freshly risked
　　　New lease of life, her fate was sealed.
NATHAN: Where is he, Daya – this heroic man?
　　　Lead me to him, pray! I must salute him!
　　　I take it that you gave him right away
　　　The cash I left with you – gave all to him?
　　　And promised him still more, far more?
DAYA:　　　　　　　　　　　　　How could we?
NATHAN: You couldn't? Didn't?
DAYA:　　　　　　　　None knew where he came
　　　from,
　　　And, when he went, we'd no idea where to.
　　　Strange to the house and led by ear alone,
　　　He boldly plunged inside with cloak outspread,
　　　Fighting his way through flames and smoke towards
　　　The voice we heard beseeching us for help.
　　　We'd given him up for lost when suddenly,
　　　From smoke and flame emerging, there he stood
　　　With Recha in his arms. Cold and unmoved
　　　By jubilant applause, he laid his booty
　　　Down and, swiftly mingling with the crowd,
　　　He disappeared!
NATHAN:　　　　　But not, I hope, for good.
DAYA: A few days later we caught sight of him
　　　Strolling to and fro beneath the palms
　　　Which shade the tomb of Christ, our Risen Lord.
　　　Delighted, I approached to thank the Knight.
　　　I praised and pleaded, begged him earnestly
　　　To grant the gentle creature sight of him,
　　　For she would not enjoy a moment's peace
　　　Until, in tears, she'd thanked her saviour.

NATHAN: Well?

DAYA: In vain. The Knight was deaf to all entreaties
  And poured on me such bitter mockery...

NATHAN: That you were frightened off...

DAYA: By no means
  so!
  Each day, I made a fresh approach to him,
  Each day, endured anew his biting scorn.
  Oh, what I didn't suffer! Yet would gladly
  Have suffered even more. He's long since ceased
  To wander in the grove of palms whose shade
  Enfolds the tomb of Christ the Resurrected.
  And nobody knows what has become of him...
  Are you amazed? You're pensive?

NATHAN: I'm reflecting
  On how a spirit sensitive as Recha's
  By such behaviour must have been cast down.
  To find herself rejected by the one
  She felt obliged most highly to esteem –
  Repulsed so brutally, yet still attracted!
  True, heart and head would long remain at odds:
  Should melancholy and misanthropy prevail?
  If neither then perhaps, imagination,
  Intervening in the strife, creates
  A dreamer, whose head now plays the heart,
  Or heart the head – a poor exchange indeed!
  Unless I'm wrong, the latter case, I think,
  Is Recha's: she's a dreamer.

DAYA: But so gentle,
  So kind-hearted!

NATHAN: Clearly, she's been smitten!

DAYA: One thing above all else is on her mind –
  A whimsy, if you will – it's that her Templar
  Is neither human, nor terrestrial, but
  The angel whose protection her young heart
  From childhood days so readily embraced,
  Descended from the clouds in which he dwells
  And, hovering about her in the flames,

Was incarnated as a Templar. Do not smile!
Or, smiling, let her cherish one illusion,
In which, at least, Jews, Christians, Moslems, too,
United stand: so sweet a fantasy!
NATHAN: And no less sweet to me! Good Daya, go –
Ask what the girl's about. I'd like a word.
I'll then seek out this moody guardian angel,
Should he be roaming yet on earth among us,
Dispensing so uncouth a chivalry.
I'm sure to find him somewhere! When I do,
I'll bring him here.
DAYA: No easy task.
NATHAN: Then shall
Sweet fantasy to reality more sweet
Give way! Believe me, Daya, flesh and blood
Mean more to any human than an angel.
So don't you blame me, don't reproach me when
You find our angel-lover has been cured.
DAYA: You are so good, but mischievous as well!
I'll go at once. But look, see! Here she comes!

Scene 2

As before, with RECHA.

RECHA: So, Father, you've returned. You're safe and sound?
I thought perhaps, you'd only sent your voice
Ahead of you. Where have you been? What mountains,
Deserts, rivers part us – even now?
You breathe the air of these four walls, yet still
You do not hurry to embrace your Recha!
Poor Recha who was nearly burned meanwhile –
Yes, almost burned alive! Not quite. Don't quake!
A ghastly way to die, being burnt alive.
NATHAN: My child! My darling child!
RECHA: You had
to cross
Euphrates, Tigris, Jordan and who knows
What other streams? How often did I tremble

For your life before the fire so nearly
Swallowed me! Since then, I've thought, to die
In water would be easeful and refreshing.
But you've not drowned, nor was I burned alive.
So let us both rejoice and praise the Lord!
You, He bore together with your ship,
Across the waves on angels' wings *unseen*;
And bade my guardian angel – *visibly* –
On *his* white wings transport me through the flames.
NATHAN: (*Aside.*)
    White wings? Why, yes! The Templar's outspread cloak.
RECHA: He bore me visibly through the fire and with
His wings beat back the flames. So I have seen
A guardian angel face to face – *my* guardian!
NATHAN: To rescue Recha was well worth his while!
    Beauty you saw in him and he, no less,
Great beauty saw in you, my darling Recha!
RECHA: (*Smiling.*)
    Whom are you flattering, Father dear? Come on:
The angel or yourself?
NATHAN: Had he been Man –
Man, such as Nature daily furnishes –
And he'd performed for you so great a service,
Then surely you'd have seen him as an angel –
An angel he both must and would have been!
RECHA: This was no human angel, but celestial!
    A real angel! Was it not you yourself
Who taught me angels possibly exist,
You who taught me God, for sake of those
Who dearly love him, miracles can work?
I do love God.
NATHAN: And He loves you; for you
And others like you, hourly wonders He
Performs and so has done for you since time
Began.
RECHA: I'm glad to hear you say so!
NATHAN: Why?
Because it might sound dull and commonplace,
Had you been rescued merely by a Templar?
Would that, in truth, be less miraculous?

The greatest miracle of all is that, to us,
True wonders, genuine miracles, become
Quite commonplace and so are meant to do.
Without that universal miracle,
Would thinking man have ever used the term
Referring to what nowadays only children
Would call a miracle, as open-mouthed,
They chase the new and strange.

DAYA: (*To NATHAN.*)   For pity's sake!
These subtleties of yours will surely snap
The child's already overburdened brain!

NATHAN: Don't interrupt! For my beloved Recha,
It isn't miracle enough that she
Was rescued by a human being whose life
Itself was saved by no small miracle!
Whoever heard of a Templar's life being spared
By Saladin? Could any Templar plead
Or hope for pardon? Still less freedom buy
With nought but leather sword-belt and a dagger?

RECHA: You've proved my case. Those are the reasons why
He wasn't what he seemed – a Templar Knight.
No captured Templar sees Jerusalem,
Unless to suffer certain death and none
Could wander freely in the city. How,
Therefore, could one, on his own, by night
Contrive my rescue?

NATHAN: Sharp – and no mistake!
Now Daya, you may speak. Twas you who told
Me he'd been sent here as a prisoner.
I do not doubt that you can tell us more.

DAYA: Indeed, that's what they say – and more besides:
That Saladin forgave the Templar Knight
Because he looked so like the Sultan's brother –
One specially beloved of Saladin.
But since the lad's been dead for twenty years –
His name and resting-place to me unknown –
The whole thing strikes me as incredible.
The story could be nothing more than gossip.

NATHAN: Why, Daya – why on earth should that be so?
What's so incredible? From time to time,

People believe things much less feasible.
Why shouldn't Saladin, who loves his people,
When younger, not have had a brother whom
He loved especially? Two faces can
Resemble one another, can they not?
Are first impressions ever lost entirely?
Does like no longer make appeal to like?
Since when? What's unbelievable about it?
For you perhaps, wise Daya, it might not
Appear miraculous, for only *yours* –
Your miracles requi– I mean, deserve belief.
DAYA: You're mocking me.
NATHAN: Do you not mock me,
too?
Be that as maybe, Recha, your salvation
Was a miracle which only He could work
Whose sport, if not his mockery, it is
On frailest threads to guide the sternest edicts
And the wildest schemes of kings.
RECHA: Dear Father!
If perchance I'm wrong, you know it's not
My wish.
NATHAN: If anything, you're keen to learn:
Foreheads, you note, are arched this way or that;
Noses, rather one way than another.
Eyebrows are straight or curved; it all depends
Whether the bone beneath is sharp or blunt.
A line, a bend, a dimple, or a mole –
A blemish on some European's face;
And you escape a fire in Asia! Are
These not miracles to people starved
Of wonders? Why involve an angel, too?
DAYA: Nathan, if I may speak my mind, what harm
If one prefers to think one's rescuer
An angel, rather than a human creature?
Wouldn't one feel thereby brought that much closer
To the intangible, prime cause of one's
Salvation?
NATHAN: Pride! That's all it is! The pot
Of iron would prefer a silver tongs

To lift it from the furnace, so that it
Can think itself, likewise, of silver wrought.
Pah! What harm? you ask. What harm, indeed?
To which I must reply in turn 'What good?'
To say, as you do, that one closer feels
To God is either nonsense or sheer blasphemy.
I say it's harmful; *that* it surely is.
Listen to me! For is it not a fact,
That you would gladly render in return
Many great services to the rescuer –
Angel or man? But were he truly angel,
What great service could you render him?
Thank him, of course, and offer sighs and prayers;
Dissolve in sheer delight at thought of him,
Fast on his feast-day and contribute alms.
All quite pointless! As it seems to me,
You and your neighbour'd profit more thereby –
Than any angel. Would your fasting serve
To fatten him? Your alms enrich him? Your
Delight his glory heighten, or your trust
His power increase? Only if he were human!

DAYA: A man would certainly have given us
More opportunity to serve *him* in some way.
And God knows very gladly we'd have done so.
However, neither wish nor need had he
For anything at all – so self-sufficient,
Self-contained, was he – as only angel
Could be.

RECHA: Finally, when he disappeared...

NATHAN: He disappeared? How so? Amid the palms
Vanished from sight, you mean? You made
No further effort then to track him down?

DAYA: Well, no, we didn't.

NATHAN: Didn't, Daya? You're
Cruel fanatics, both of you! What if
This angel had – for instance – fallen ill?

RECHA: Ill?

DAYA: He couldn't!

RECHA: I grow cold with dread –

Daya, feel my forehead! Warm before,
Now suddenly, it's icy –
NATHAN: After all,
He's a Frank – a stranger to our climate;
He's young, unused to hunger, lack of sleep
The rigours of a soldier's life.
RECHA: Ill! Ill!
DAYA: Nathan is only saying that it could be so.
NATHAN: And there he'd lie with neither friend nor gold
To buy him friends in need.
RECHA: Oh, father dear!
NATHAN: Without a roof – without advice or contact,
A helpless prey to pain, a prey to death!
RECHA: Where? Where?
NATHAN: He who, for one he did not
know,
Had never seen – enough, it was a human –
Yet braved the fire…
DAYA: Have pity on her, Nathan!
NATHAN: Who neither wished to know or see the one
He'd rescued, so that she'd not feel obliged
To him…
DAYA: Oh, Nathan, spare her!
NATHAN: Nor desired
Ever to set eyes on her again unless
He had to rescue her a second time –
A human after all…
DAYA: Stop! Look!
NATHAN: Now, dying, he's no comfort to refresh him,
Nought save the knowledge of that deed!
DAYA: Enough!
You're killing her!
NATHAN: And you have killed the Knight –
Or clearly could have done so. Recha! Recha!
It's medicine I'm offering you, not poison.
He's alive! Come to your senses! He's not dead;
Not even ill!
RECHA: You're sure? Not dead? Not ill?

NATHAN: Not dead, I'm sure! For God rewards good deeds,
    Even on earth. What you must understand
    Is how much easier is reverential zeal
    Than virtuous action! Gladly the idlest man
    Adores with pious zeal in order – though
    Unconscious of his aim – to spare himself
    The opportunity for action –
RECHA: Oh,
    Father! Please don't ever leave your Recha
    Alone again! You mean to say that he
    May just have gone away?
NATHAN: Of course, why not?
    I see a Moslem curiously eyeing
    My laden camels. Do you know the man?
DAYA: It's your Dervish.
NATHAN: Who?
DAYA: Your chess companion!
NATHAN: Al Hafi? That Al Hafi?
DAYA: Now the Sultan's
    Treasurer.
NATHAN: What? Al Hafi? Am I dreaming?
    It is, it's really him! And coming here.
    Quick! Inside, the pair of you! What now?

Scene 3

NATHAN and the Dervish AL HAFI.

AL HAFI: Yes, open your eyes as wide as they will go!
NATHAN: Can it be you? So splendidly attired!
    A Dervish!
AL HAFI: Why not? Is a Dervish, then,
    By his very nature good for nothing?
NATHAN: I don't say that! It's only that I thought
    A proper Dervish – vows and that – would not
    Accept advancement.
AL HAFI: By the Prophet! I
    Grant you, I am not the most devout,
    But when needs must –

NATHAN: Needs must? A Dervish must?
  No man is forced to be obliged! What then
  Compels a Dervish?
AL HAFI: If he's kindly asked
  And sees the point, why then, a Dervish must!
NATHAN: By the God we share, you're talking sense
  Let me embrace you, man! You're still my friend?
AL HAFI: First, don't you want to know what I've become?
NATHAN: No matter what!
AL HAFI: But if I chanced to be
  A servant of the State whose friendship might
  Embarrass you, what then?
NATHAN: If you're at heart
  Still Dervish, I will risk it! Uniform
  Alone makes you official –
AL HAFI: But demands
  Respect as well. Consider! In your home,
  What would I be?
NATHAN: A Dervish – nothing more.
  Or, possibly – a cook besides.
AL HAFI: You see!
  With you, my skills would go to waste! A cook!?
  Not butler, too? You'll grant that Saladin
  Knows better… I'm his Treasurer…
NATHAN: What, you?
AL HAFI: Master, that is, of the Sultan's household Purse.
  His father is still Treasurer of State.
NATHAN: The household's large –
AL HAFI: Far larger than
  you think
  For every beggar here's the Sultan's guest.
NATHAN: Yet Saladin is so opposed to beggars –
AL HAFI: So much so that he plans to rid the land
  Of them – yes, root and branch – albeit he'll
  Be beggared in the process!
NATHAN: As I thought!
AL HAFI: He's good as ruined now. His Treasury
  With every passing day is emptier
  Than empty, for the morning tide of income,

Long before noon, has swiftly turned about
And ebbed –
NATHAN: In part consumed by channels which
Can no more be effectively replenished
Than they can be blocked up again…
AL HAFI: Precisely.
NATHAN: Well I know it!
AL HAFI: Simply will not do
For princes to be vultures amid carrion –
But ten times worse, if they are to become
Carrion amid vultures.
NATHAN: Dervish, God forbid!
Don't say such things!
AL HAFI: All right for you to talk!
What would you give me to resign my post
To you?
NATHAN: How much does it bring in?
AL HAFI: To me?
Not much. But it could nicely swell your coffers.
For when the tide is low, as often happens,
You'd open up your sluices, lend your cash,
And charge whatever interest you see fit.
NATHAN: Then, interest on the interest and so on?
AL HAFI: Why not?
NATHAN: Till all my capital is gone?
AL HAFI: Not tempted? Then, we might as well agree
To end our friendship here and now, for I
Was counting on your full support.
NATHAN: How so?
In what respect?
AL HAFI: I thought you'd help me gain
Distinction in my office since your cash
Has hitherto been at my beck and call.
You shake your head?
NATHAN: Let's get this straight, my
friend!
There is a difference here. For you, yourself,
Why not? Al Hafi Dervish is as ever

Welcome to all assistance I can offer.
Al Hafi, though, as Sultan's Treasurer,
Who to –
AL HAFI: There! I might have guessed! You're still as good
As you are shrewd, and shrewd as you are wise.
Patience! The paradox which you perceive in me
Will shortly be resolved. Look at this robe
Of honour, given to me by Saladin.
Before it's worn away to rags and tatters,
And fitting raiment for a Dervish, I'll
Have left it hanging in Jerusalem
While by the Ganges, barefoot and serene,
The hot sand I'll be treading with my teachers.
NATHAN: That's more like you!
AL HAFI: Playing chess with
them.
NATHAN: Your greatest joy!
AL HAFI: You wonder what
seduced me?
The thought of never needing more to beg?
Of playing rich man to the pauper throng?
Of being able in a trice to turn
The richest beggar to a poor man's Croesus?
NATHAN: That, I doubt!
AL HAFI: The lure was far less subtle!
I felt flattered for the first time ever –
By the Sultan's kindly whim…
NATHAN: Which was?
AL HAFI: 'Only a beggar knows how beggars feel,'
He told me. 'Only one who's begged himself
Knows how to give and yet not give offence.
Your predecessor was too cold, too clumsy.
When he gave, he gave ungraciously,
Investigating the recipient.
Not content to know the need existed,
He'd always question how it came about,
In order stingily to calculate
What alms he need reluctantly dispense.

You won't do that, for Saladin must not
Appear through you a lukewarm benefactor,
Nor must Al Hafi seem like some blocked pipe
Which pure, still water having taken in,
Releases it in turbid dribs and drabs.
I know,' he said, 'you think and feel as I do.'
Thus sweetly did the charmer play his pipe,
Till I, the gull, was well and truly gulled.
Me! Tricked by a trickster!

NATHAN: Easy, Dervish!
Easy!

AL HAFI: Wouldn't you call it trickery –
Men by the hundred thousand to oppress,
Starve, plunder, torture, scourge and strangle,
While lavishing your favours on a few?
Not trickery – without the All-Highest's ever
Bounteous hand, to seek to ape divine
Compassion which, regardless of good or evil,
Desert or plain, in sunshine or in rain,
Embraces all? Is that not trickery?

NATHAN: Stop! Enough!

AL HAFI: Let me at least confess
My own hypocrisy. Was it not such,
To search his trickery for a trace of virtue,
To justify myself in sharing his
Deceit? Was that not also trickery?

NATHAN: Al Hafi, lose no time but hasten back
Into your wilderness, for I'm afraid
That, here among men, you may perhaps forget
How to be human.

AL HAFI: Yes, I fear as much.
Farewell!

NATHAN: So suddenly? No wait, Al Hafi!
Your desert sands won't run away! Hold hard!
Don't think he hears me – Hi, Al Hafi, wait!
He's gone and I would very much have liked
To question him about the Templar Knight.
He might well know him.

Scene 4

Enter DAYA hurriedly.

DAYA: Nathan, Nathan!
NATHAN: Yes?
What is it?
DAYA: He has reappeared! We've just
Caught sight of him!
NATHAN: Who, Daya, who?
DAYA: Him! He!
NATHAN: Him? He? Who do you mean? Has he no name?
To call him only 'he' is rather rude –
Even if he were, in fact, an angel!
DAYA: He's walking to and fro among the palms,
Plucking himself a date from time to time.
NATHAN: And eating it – just like a Templar?
DAYA: Must
You tease me? Her keen eye at once divined
Twas he, despite the interlocking fronds,
And followed him intently. Now she asks -
She begs you, go to him at once! Please hurry!
She says she'll signal to you from her window
Which path he's taking – to'ards us, or away.
Make haste!
NATHAN: Like this? Still dressed for camel-back?
Would that be fitting? Rather you go out
And tell him I've returned. It's natural
An honest man would wish to shun my home
While I'm away. But now I'm back and he's
Invited by none other than her father,
He'll be glad to come. Say I request –
Most heartily invite…
DAYA: No use! He won't
Accept. He'd never call on any Jew.
NATHAN: Go, nonetheless, and try to hold him there,
Your eyes, at least, will keep him company.
Go you and I shall follow you directly.
(NATHAN hurries indoors and DAYA sets off.)

Scene 5

A square with palms under which the TEMPLAR is strolling to and fro. Following him, at a slight remove, is a LAY-BROTHER who seems anxious to speak to him.

TEMPLAR: It can't be boredom keeps him at my heels –
　　The way he steals a look from time to time.
　　Good Brother – or perhaps I should say Father?
BROTHER: Brother – I'm a layman – at your service.
TEMPLAR:　　　Brother, if I had anything to give –
　　God's truth, I've nothing –
BROTHER:　　　　　　　　Yes, you have –
　　My warmest gratitude. God will repay
　　A thousandfold what you would wish to give.
　　The will and not the gift proclaims the giver.
　　In any case, I was not sent to pester
　　You for alms.
TEMPLAR:　　　　But you *were* sent to me?
BROTHER:　　　Yes, from the monastery.
TEMPLAR:　　　　　　　　　　Where I had
　　hoped
　　I might enjoy a pilgrim's scant repast.
BROTHER: The tables were all taken but do, please,
　　Come back once more with me.
TEMPLAR:　　　　　　　　What for?
　　It's ages, true, since I last tasted meat;
　　What matter, though? These dates are fully ripe.
BROTHER: You must be careful sampling this fruit.
　　It isn't wise to eat too many dates.
　　They clog the spleen, spread melancholy humours.
TEMPLAR: And what if I prefer being melancholy?
　　I don't suppose this warning was the reason
　　You were sent to see me?
BROTHER:　　　　　　No, indeed!
　　I'm here for information, as it were,
　　To sound you out.
TEMPLAR:　　　　You don't mind telling me?

BROTHER: Why not?

TEMPLAR: (*Aside.*)   A crafty Brother this! (*Aloud.*) Are there
More like you in the monastery?

BROTHER: Don't know.
I just obey my orders.

TEMPLAR: Which you do
Without too closely questioning their content?

BROTHER: It wouldn't be obedience if I did.

TEMPLAR: (*Aside.*) Simplicity is always in the right!
(*Aloud.*) No doubt you're also ready to confide
Who wants to know a little more about me.
I'd swear it's not yourself.

BROTHER: Would that become me?
What would be the point?

TEMPLAR: Then who would gain
By being that curious about me? Who!

BROTHER: The Patriarch, I must assume. For he it was
Who sent me here.

TEMPLAR: The Patriarch himself?
Doesn't he know the red cross on white tunic
Better than to –

BROTHER: *I* do!

TEMPLAR: Come, Brother, come!
I am a Templar and a prisoner
Who, may I add, was captured at Tebnin,
The fort which, just before the truce expired,
We planned to storm and thence without delay
Advance on Sidon. I might also add:
Of twenty Templars captured there, I was
The only one whose life the Sultan spared.
And that is all the Patriarch needs to know;
More, in fact.

BROTHER: Yet hardly anything
He doesn't know already. For example,
He'd like to know why you alone were pardoned
By Sultan Saladin.

TEMPLAR: As if I knew!
I'd bared my neck and knelt upon my cloak

To wait the blow when Sultan Saladin
Looked hard at me, sprang forward, gave a sign.
They lifted me and freed me from my shackles.
The Sultan was in tears. I meant to thank him.
But, silent, he withdrew and left me standing.
What all of that may mean, the Patriarch
Himself had best decipher.

BROTHER: He assumes
That God must have decided to preserve you
For greater things to come.

TEMPLAR: Such greater things
As saving a Jewish maiden from a fire –
Escorting curious pilgrims on their way
To Sinai – and so on?

BROTHER: There's more to come.
Meanwhile, the prospects are encouraging.
It may be that the Patriarch himself
Already has in mind some great assignment.

TEMPLAR: You think so, Brother? Has he given you
Some hint of what it is?

BROTHER: Indeed he has!
I am instructed first to sound you out,
To see if you're his man.

TEMPLAR: Then, sound me out.
(*Aside.*) I wonder how he'll go about it! (*Aloud.*) Well?

BROTHER: Simplest perhaps if I explain to you,
Without ado, the Patriarch's desires.

TEMPLAR: Please
do.

BROTHER: He'd like to send a letter
By your hand.

TEMPLAR: By me? I'm not a messenger!
Think you that such an enterprise would be
More glorious than rescuing a Jewish maiden
From a fire?

BROTHER: Presumably – for so
The Patriarch avers – upon this letter
Will depend the fate of Christendom.

Safe conduct of the letter, so he says,
God will reward one day in paradise
With a hero's crown of quite outstanding merit.
There's none more worthy, says the Patriarch,
Of such an honour than yourself.
TEMPLAR: Than I?
BROTHER: None more aptly skilled or better placed
Deservedly to win this golden crown
Than you, sir, says the Patriarch.
TEMPLAR: Than I?
BROTHER: You're free to wander where you will,
Surveying all, so says the Patriarch;
You know how to storm a city and protect it;
You can assess the strengths and weaknesses
Of Saladin's new second, inner wall,
And best describe it in the clearest terms
To those who struggle in the cause of God.
That's what he said.
TEMPLAR: Good Brother, I would like
To know this letter's content in more detail.
BROTHER: As to that, I don't know all the facts.
The letter is addressed to French King Phillip.
I've often wondered how the Patriarch –
A holy man who lives so much in heaven –
Can condescend to keep so well abreast
Of earthly matters. Must be hard for him.
TEMPLAR: The Patriarch, you mean?
BROTHER: Knows
everything:
Reliably informed both how and where
And in what strength and whence the Sultan
His campaign will launch, in the event
That war breaks out anew.
TEMPLAR: He knows?
BROTHER: He does
And would inform King Phillip, so that he
Can make a sound assessment whether we
Face dangers such, we'd best – at any cost –
Restore at once the truce with Saladin,
So valiantly broken by your Order.

TEMPLAR: What a Patriarch! The dear, brave man,
It seems, would have me be no common envoy
But – a spy! So, Brother, you may go
And tell your Patriarch, as far as you've
Been able to assess, it's not for me!
Say I regard myself as still a prisoner.
Moreover, tell him that a Templar's sole
Vocation is to wield the sword and not
To play the spy. That's all!

BROTHER: Just as I thought!
Forgive me, I don't blame you in the least:
The best is yet to come! The Patriarch
Has ferreted out the name and situation
Of the fort in Lebanon in which are stored
Huge sums the Sultan's prudent father uses
To pay the troops and buy the tools of war.
From time to time, the Sultan on his own,
Almost unguarded, by a secret route,
Visits this stronghold, so –

TEMPLAR: Not on your life!

BROTHER: What could be easier than to overpower
The Sultan and then do him in? You flinch?
Why, a couple of God-fearing Marionites
Have volunteered already. All they need
Is some brave man prepared to risk his neck
And take command.

TEMPLAR: No doubt the Patriarch
Has also chosen me as that brave man?

BROTHER: He thinks that Philip King of France would be
Best placed to lend a helping hand from Acre –

TEMPLAR: A helping hand to me? Why *me*, good Brother?
Haven't you heard? Or heard it only now –
The debt I owe to Saladin?

BROTHER: I know.

TEMPLAR: Well, then?

BROTHER: The Patriarch's view is: that's all well and good,
But God and the Order…

TEMPLAR: Make no difference!
I'll not be guilty of a knavish trick!
BROTHER: Just so!
A knavish trick in man's eyes it may seem;
But, says the Patriarch, not so in God's.
TEMPLAR: I owe my life to Saladin. Should I
Now rob him of his own?
BROTHER: The Patriarch
Says, since the Sultan's still the foe
Of Christianity, he has no right
To claim your friendship.
TEMPLAR: Friend or not –
I'll not behave towards him like a scoundrel –
A thankless one at that!
BROTHER: Quite so, but still,
The Patriarch maintains we owe no thanks
To God or man for service not requested.
He therefore argues that, since rumour has it,
The Sultan only pardoned you because
Something about your manner or your bearing
Reminded him in some way of his brother...
TEMPLAR: Your Patriarch knows that as well, does he?
Oh, would that much were certain! Saladin!
If Nature in my looks combined *one* trait
Expressive of your brother's character,
Would it not chime with something in my soul?
And that relationship would I suppress
Merely to satisfy a Patriarch?
Nature does not lie, nor in Creation
Does God so contradict Himself! Go, Brother!
Don't make me lose my temper! Go, at once!
BROTHER: I'm going – happier now than when I came.
Forgive me, sir, but we monastic folk

Must do as we are told by those above us.

Scene 6

The TEMPLAR and DAYA who, after observing him for some time, now approaches.

DAYA: (*Aside.*) I rather think the Brother left him not
    In the best of moods! No matter, nonetheless,
    I will attempt my mission!
TEMPLAR: Marvellous!
    The proverb's right enough: that monk and woman,
    Woman and monk, are the talons of the Devil.
    Today, he's tossing me from one to t'other.
DAYA: Noble Knight, it's you! Thanks be to God!
    A thousand thanks, indeed! Where have you been
    For so long past? I only hope that you
    Have not been ill?
TEMPLAR: No.
DAYA: You've been well then?
TEMPLAR:
    Yes.
DAYA: Good. We'd begun to worry seriously
    On your behalf.
TEMPLAR: Indeed.
DAYA: Were you away?
TEMPLAR: You've guessed aright.
DAYA: Just back?
TEMPLAR: No,
    yesterday.
DAYA: Recha's father, too, came home today.
    So now, perhaps, may Recha hope for –
TEMPLAR: What?
DAYA: The meeting she so often has requested.
    Her father, Nathan, pressingly invites you
    To visit them. He's come from Babylon
    With twenty camels laden heavily
    With all the Orient's most precious goods –

Gems, silks and valuables of every kind
That India, Persia, Syria, even China
Have to offer.
TEMPLAR: Never buy a thing!
DAYA: He's honoured by his people like a prince.
Though, why they always label him 'the Wise',
Instead of 'Rich', has often puzzled me.
TEMPLAR: Wise and rich perhaps are much the same
In people's eyes.
DAYA: By rights he should be known
As the Good; you can't imagine, sir,
How good he is. The moment he heard the debt
That Recha owed, there's nothing he would not
Have done for you or given!
TEMPLAR: Is that so?
DAYA: Come try it! See for yourself!
TEMPLAR: See what?
How soon such moment passes?
DAYA: Were he not
As good as I have said, would I have stayed
So long with him? Do you suppose I'm not
Aware of my true value as a Christian?
I'd no idea that I was following
My spouse to Palestine to educate
A Jewish girl. My noble husband rode
With Kaiser Frederick's cavalry –
TEMPLAR: And he
Was born a Swiss and had the grace and honour
With His Imperial Majesty to drown
In a river and so on. How many times
Have you already told me all of that?
Why will you not stop following me about?
DAYA: Following, dear God!
TEMPLAR: Yes, following me.
I just don't want to see you any more!
Nor hear you! I don't want repeatedly
To be reminded of a deed which I
Performed without a second thought, which, when

I ponder, leaves me puzzled at myself.
It's not that I regret it. Nonetheless,
Should such an incident occur again,
You'd be to blame, were I to act less swiftly,
First investigate and then decide
To let what's burning burn.

DAYA: Oh, God forbid!

TEMPLAR: Do me at least the favour from today
Of leaving me alone, I beg of you.
Don't let her father near me. Jews are Jews.
I'm just a simple Swabian. That girl
Has long since vanished from my thoughts –
If ever there!

DAYA: But she remembers you!

TEMPLAR: Why should she? What's the point?

DAYA: Who
knows?
People aren't always what they seem to be.

TEMPLAR: But seldom any better. (*He walks away.*)

DAYA: Wait a moment!
Why rush off?

TEMPLAR: Woman, don't make me hate
This palm-grove, where I so much like to stroll.

DAYA: Then go, you German bear! Be on your way!
(*Aside.*) Mustn't lose track of the creature, all the same!
(*She follows him at a distance.*)

End of Act One.

ACT TWO

Scene 1

The Sultan's Palace.

SALADIN and SITTAH playing chess.

SITTAH: Saladin, your mind's not on the game!
SALADIN: Wrong move? A good one, I'd have said.
SITTAH:
　For me!
　There, take it back.
SALADIN:　　　　　　　Why?
SITTAH:　　　　　　　　　You have left your
　Knight
　Exposed.
SALADIN: So I have. What of it?
SITTAH:　　　　　　　　　I can fork
　Your pieces.
SALADIN:　　True again. Then I cry 'check!'
SITTAH: What good is that? While I advance,
　You're stuck.
SALADIN:　　There's no way out for me, I see
　Without some sacrifice. Just take my Knight.
SITTAH: I could but as it happens, I don't want him.
　I'll pass.
SALADIN: I see you're doing me no favour;
　You've bigger fish to fry than just a Knight.
SITTAH: Could be.
SALADIN: But you had better think again, my dear.
　Look out! I'll bet you weren't expecting that!
SITTAH: I wasn't, true. But how was I to guess
　That you would weary of your Queen so
　Early on!
SALADIN:　Me weary of my Queen?
SITTAH: It's clear today I'll win my thousand dinars

And not a measly silver nickel more.

SALADIN: How so?

SITTAH: Why ask? Because you seem determined,
By hook or crook, to lose. But that was not
What I was counting on. Besides the fact
That such a game is not so entertaining,
Didn't I always gain by being defeated?
You never failed to offer consolation
By giving me twice the stake as my reward.

SALADIN: So when you lost a game you had good reason
To lose with all your heart, my little sister!

SITTAH: At least, it might be argued, little brother,
That your own generosity's to blame
If I've not learned to play more skilfully.

SALADIN: We're losing sight of the game. Let's finish it!

SITTAH: So be it! Check and check again, I cry.

SALADIN: Too true, my dear. That move I didn't see;
I've lost my King and lost my Queen as well!

SITTAH: Could something have been done to save the day?
Let's see!

SALADIN: No, no. Have done and take my Queen.
That piece has never brought me any luck.

SITTAH: Only the piece?

SALADIN: Away with her! It makes
No difference. Everything's protected
Once again.

SITTAH: My brother's taught me only all
Too well the courtesy to which a Queen's
Entitled. (*She does not remove it.*)

SALADIN: Take her or let her be! I have
None left.

SITTAH: But what's the point of taking her?
Check! Check!

SALADIN: Get on with it!

SITTAH: Check, check and check!

SALADIN: Then mate!

SITTAH: Not quite. You still can move
your
       Knight.
It's up to you. It doesn't really matter.

SALADIN: Quite right. You've won the match. Al Hafi pays.
Where is he? Have him brought to me at once.
What you were saying, Sittah, was quite right:
I wasn't concentrating on the game.
Who keeps giving us this set of gem-stones?
They don't remind one of the normal chess-men,
So have no meaning. After all, I wasn't playing
With the Imam. Defeat demands excuses. But
In truth, these shapeless pieces weren't the reason
That I lost: it was your skill and cunning,
Sittah – your astuteness – cool and swift.
SITTAH: You're trying to blunt the barb of your defeat;
Enough, you were distracted more than I.
SALADIN: Than *you?* What was distracting *you?*
SITTAH:
Not your
Distractions, I agree. Oh, Saladin,
When shall we play so seriously again?
SALADIN: All the more ardently, when we get the chance!
Another conflict is about to start, you think.
Well, let it! I was not the first to march.
The truce I'd gladly have extended yet again
And gladly would have seen my Sittah wed
A worthy husband: Richard's brother, yes –
He's Richard's brother, therefore must be worthy.
SITTAH: You never cease to sing your Richard's praises!
SALADIN: Were Richard's sister to espouse our brother,
Melek, what a dynasty we'd found!
The first and finest royal house on earth!
I am not slow to praise myself, you note.
I think I'm worthy of my friends. But oh,
What men such union would produce! What humans!
SITTAH: Did I not mock that vision from the start?
The Christians you don't know, nor wish to know.
Their pride is in being Christian, not human.
Even that which since their Founder's day,
Has spiced their superstition with humanity,
They do not love because it's human, but

Because Christ taught it and for what he did.
They're lucky he was such a paragon;
That they can take his virtue so for granted!
What virtue, though? Not virtue but his name
Is what they spread abroad by force to smirch
And devour the names of all good men.
So far as they're concerned, the name – the name –
Is all that matters.

SALADIN: You don't think they might
Have other reasons for insisting you
And Melek first accept their faith so as
To love your Christian spouses worthily.

SITTAH: It's as though Christians only, they alone,
Have any right to the love with which
The Creator has endowed each man and woman.

SALADIN: Christians believe so many paltry myths,
It wouldn't trouble them to swallow that as well.
And yet you are mistaken. Templars – not
Christians – are at fault; and not as Christians
But as Templars. They're responsible
For wrecking all our hopes. They won't let go
Of Acre, the port which Richard's sister was
To bring our brother Melek as her dowry.
In order not to risk their Knights' advantage,
They're sticking by their stupid monkish rules
While hoping, as Knights to take us by surprise,
They strike before expiry of our truce.
Splendid, gentlemen! If that's your style,
Proceed as you've begun. I'll not object!
If only other matters –

SITTAH: For example?
What else is there to worry you? What else
Could plague you so?

SALADIN: The same old thing
That never yet has failed to irritate me.
I've just been in the Lebanon with our father.
He's overcome with worries –

SITTAH: What a shame!

SALADIN: He cannot cope; there's holdups everywhere;
    Recurrent shortages –
SITTAH: What of? What's wrong?
SALADIN: What else, save what I hardly deign to mention?
    When I have it, I can do without it,
    But when I lack it, then it seems essential.
    What's Al Hafi doing? Was he sent for?
    Where is he? What a curse, confounded money!
    Ah, good! At last, Al Hafi!

Scene 2

AL HAFI, SALADIN, SITTAH.

AL HAFI: Cash from Egypt
    Has presumably arrived. I only hope
    There's plenty of it!
SALADIN: Have you news?
AL HAFI: Not I –
    I thought you'd some to give me.
SALADIN: Pay to Sittah
    One thousand dinars! (*Walking to and fro, thinking.*)
AL HAFI: Pay – and not collect!
    I like that! Less than nothing in the till!!
    Pay Sittah? Sittah yet again? You've lost
    At chess? The game's still there!
SITTAH: You'll grant me
    My good fortune?
AL HAFI: (*Studying the game.*) I should grant you? But
    You know quite well –
SITTAH: (*Signalling.*)   Oh, hush, Al Hafi, hush!
AL HAFI: (*Eyes still on the board.*)
    First grant it to yourself!
SITTAH: Hush, Hafi, hush!
AL HAFI: (*To SITTAH.*)
    The Whites were yours? You offered 'check'.
SITTAH: It's good he didn't hear.
AL HAFI: His turn to move?
SITTAH: (*Closer to him.*) Al Hafi, just assure me if you please

That I'll receive the money owed –

AL HAFI: (*Still concentrating on the board.*) You will –
You'll get it, as you've never failed to do.

SITTAH: What? Are you mad?

AL HAFI: The game is not yet
won.
You haven't been defeated, Saladin.

SALADIN: (*Hardly listening.*)
Yes, I have! Pay up, pay up!

AL HAFI: Pay up!?
Your Queen is still in play.

SALADIN: (*Abstracted.*)   No, no she's not!
She's out of it!

SITTAH: That's it, then; say
That I may now collect the cash I've won.

AL HAFI: (*Still concentrating on the game.*)
Of course, as always. Even though the Queen
May count no longer, Saladin, you've still
Not been checkmated.

SALADIN: (*Steps forward and overturns the board.*)
                                                   Yes, I have and that's
My wish.

AL HAFI: I see! To hell with game and stake!
No sooner won than paid.

SALADIN: (*To SITTAH.*)   What's that he says?

SITTAH: (*Signalling to AL HAFI from time to time.*)
You know what he's like. He always plays reluctant.
Likes to be begged, and envious, as well.

SALADIN: Not of my sister, surely? Not my sister!
What's this, Hafi? Envious? You?

AL HAFI: Could be.
Perhaps. I only wish I had her brain!
And I'd be glad if I could match her kindness.

SITTAH: But up to now he's always paid correctly
And he will pay today. Just give him time.
Go now, Al Hafi, go. I'll send a servant
To collect the cash.

AL HAFI: Enough of this charade!
I'll play no longer. High time that he learnt
The truth.
SALADIN: Who and what about?
SITTAH: Al Hafi!
What did you promise me? This is no way
To keep your word?
AL HAFI: But how was I to know
That things would go this far?
SALADIN: What *is* all this?
SITTAH: I beg of you, Al Hafi – be discreet!
SALADIN: It's very strange! What can it be that Sittah
Prefers to ask with so much pomp and ardour
Of a Dervish outsider, rather than her brother?
Al Hafi, this is an order: Dervish, speak!
SITTAH: Don't let a trifle, brother, bother you
More than it deserves. As well you know,
At various times I've won the same amount
From you while playing chess. Because I had
No need of cash at present and because
Money's not all that plentiful in Hafi's chest,
I left it where it was. But do not fret!
That's not to say I'm giving it to you,
Or Hafi or indeed his treasury.
AL HAFI: If that were only so!
SITTAH: And more besides –
Was left to languish in the chest,
Allowances for court expenses, too,
I haven't touched these past months –
AL HAFI: And
that's
Not all.
SALADIN: More still? Come, out with it, Al Hafi!
AL HAFI: While we've been waiting for Egyptian gold,
She has –
SITTAH: (*To SALADIN.*) Why listen?
AL HAFI: Not received a
cent –

SALADIN: Dear sister! Then you, too, have been advancing
    Funds, it seems –
AL HAFI: Supporting all the Court
    On nothing but her personal allowance
    From yourself.
SALADIN: She has? My dear, good sister!
    (*He embraces her.*)
SITTAH: Who else made me so rich that I could do it,
    But you yourself, my brother?
AL HAFI: And he'll very
    Soon reduce her, like himself, to
    Beggardom.
SALADIN: Me, poor? My brother, poor?
    When have I had more than now? When less?
    A cloak, a sword, a horse, a God to worship!
    What more do I need? For He will never fail me.
    But you, Al Hafi, you I could reproach.
SITTAH: Don't scold him, brother. If I only could
    Have lightened father's burden from my purse!
SALADIN: There! Now once again you've brought my soaring
    Spirits down to earth! For my part, I
    Lack nothing and need fear no lack. But he –
    He lacks so much and we all share it with him.
    What am I to do? We may get nothing
    From Egypt for a long time yet, God only knows
    The reason, since things there are quiet still.
    I'll gladly curb my lifestyle, cut expenses
    Provided no one suffers but myself.
    What difference, however, will that make?
    A horse, a cloak, a sword – those I must keep.
    Nor can I afford to part with God.
    Already He makes do with very little:
    Only my heart… Al Hafi, you must know
    That I'd been counting on the surplus from
    Your treasury.
AL HAFI: Surplus, you say! Admit as much,
    You would have had me skewered or at least
    Strangled, had you caught me with a surplus!
    Embezzlement! As though I'd dare!
SALADIN: Well, then,

What shall we do? Could you find no one else
To borrow from but Sittah?
SITTAH: Would I allow
A privilege so great to be denied me?
Me by him? I still insist upon it.
Even now, I have a little left.
SALADIN: A little only!
That bad, is it? Al Hafi go arrange a loan
At once, from anyone and any way.
Go out and borrow. Promise. But don't take
From those whom I've made rich, for that would seem
Like asking them to hand their fortune back.
Seek out great misers; they'll be glad to lend,
Knowing their gold will flourish in my hands.
AL HAFI: I don't know any.
SITTAH: Just occurred to me:
I hear that friend of yours is back.
AL HAFI: (*Nonplussed.*)   What friend?
Who do you mean?
SITTAH: The Jew you praise so highly.
AL HAFI: Me? Highly praise a Jew?
SITTAH: Well I
remember
Still the phrase you used – a Jew on whom
God had heaped in fullest measure two
Treasures of this world, greatest and least.
AL HAFI: Did I say that? Whatever did I mean?
SITTAH: Wealth is the least; the greatest treasure – wisdom.
AL HAFI: Were those my words? About a Jew, you say?
SITTAH: Come, come! Was that not what you said about
Your Nathan?
AL HAFI: Him! Why, yes! I wasn't thinking!
It's true, is it, that he's returned at last?
If so, he can't be doing all that badly.
'Nathan the Wise,' they used to call him,
Or 'The Rich'.
SITTAH: 'The Rich' they call him now
Far more than ever. The town is full of talk.
The valuables, ornaments and precious goods
He's brought.
AL HAFI: Well, now that he is rich again,

93

Wise he will also be once more.
SITTAH: Al Hafi,
How would it be, were you to go and see him?
AL HAFI: What for? No hope of borrowing! You know
What Nathan's like. A loan from him!
The essence of his wisdom is 'don't lend!'
SITTAH: The picture you painted of him in my mind
Was very different.
AL HAFI: If need be, goods
He might lend – as for money – never, ever!
Nathan's a Jew but there aren't many like him:
Broad-minded, knows how to live and plays good chess.
In times both good and bad, he is outstanding
Among all other Jews. But do not count on him.
He gives to the poor, it's true – like Saladin –
If less, at least, he gives as freely, and
With no more fuss. As Nathan sees it,
Jews and Christians, Moslems, Farsees – all
Are one.
SITTAH: And such a man...
SALADIN: How can it be
That I have never even heard of him?
SITTAH: And he'd not lend, you say, to Saladin,
Whose need is all for others, not himself?
AL HAFI: That's where the Jew in him shows through;
At heart, a very ordinary Jew! Believe me!
He's jealous of your generosity;
So envious, all gratitude for gifts
He covets for himself alone. That's why
He never lends, so making sure he always has
Enough to give away. While he must give
According to the law, he isn't bound by law
To joy in doing so. Thus, charity makes
Him the least congenial of fellow-men.
For some time now, relations have been strained
Between the pair of us, but don't imagine
That, therefore, I would be unjust to him.
He's one of the best but not in that respect –
No, not in that particular. I'll go
And knock at other doors... There is a Moor

Who just now comes to mind, a wealthy miser.
I'll go at once – I'll go and seek him out.
SITTAH: What's the hurry?
SALADIN: Let him go!

Scene 3

SITTAH and SALADIN.

SITTAH: He fled
As though delighted to escape from me!
I wonder why! Did Nathan really play
Him false, or is Al Hafi's true intent
To cheat the pair of us?
SALADIN: I've no idea.
I hardly knew whom you were both discussing.
First time, indeed, I ever heard your Nathan
Mentioned.
SITTAH: How could Nathan ever have escaped
Your notice? A man of whom it's said that he
Discovered the tombs of Solomon and David –
Thanks to his knowledge of some powerful,
Occult spell which helped him break the seals.
From these, they say, he brings to light,
From time to time, riches immeasurable
No lesser source could yield.
SALADIN: If Nathan's treasures
Stem from tombs, they can't be Solomon's
Or David's, for in those two sepulchres,
Fools lie buried!
SITTAH: Fools or miscreants!
Besides, the source of Nathan's boundless wealth
Is richer far, more inexhaustible,
Than any charnel treasure-trove.
SALADIN: A merchant?
SITTAH: His camel-trains traverse all routes and trails,
Cross every desert and his vessels lie
At anchor in all ports. That much Al Hafi
Told me earlier, with delight recounting
To what great and noble use his friend
Puts all he rates it worth his merchant skill

And industry to garner; stressed moreover,
How free of prejudice was Nathan's soul,
How open his frank heart to every virtue,
How much in tune with all that's beautiful.
SALADIN: Yet Hafi just now sounded so uncertain,
So cold towards him.
SITTAH: I would say embarrassed,
Fearing it might be dangerous to praise him,
While anxious not to criticise unfairly.
Could it perhaps be that the best of Jews
Can still not quite escape his race and that
Al Hafi therefore feels a twinge of shame
To count him as his friend? That's up to him!
Whether this Nathan's more a Jew or less –
Who cares? Provided he is rich, he'll do!
SALADIN: But, sister, you would surely not approve
Of using force to take what's his?
SITTAH: Depends
What you call force. Not fire and sword!
To move the weak, what need for greater force
Than their own weakness? Come to my harem
And hear a singer I bought yesterday.
Meanwhile, I have a little scheme in mind
For getting round this Nathan. Come along!

Scene 4

*In front of Nathan's house, bordering on the palm-grove. RECHA
and NATHAN emerge, shortly joined by DAYA.*

RECHA: Father, you took so long to get here, you've
Little chance of meeting him.
NATHAN: Come now,
Perhaps if not just here among the palms,
Well, somewhere else. Hush now! Is that not Daya
Making her way towards us?
RECHA: So it is.
I'm sure she must have lost him.
NATHAN: Maybe not.

RECHA: Otherwise she wouldn't just be dawdling.

NATHAN: Probably hasn't seen us.

RECHA: Now, she has!

NATHAN: And she's begun to hurry, hasn't she?
    Contain yourself! Be patient!

RECHA: Father, would you
    Really want a daughter who was patient –
    Indifferent to the man whose act of mercy
    Saved her life? A life so dear to her
    Not least because she owes it first to you.

NATHAN: I wouldn't have you other than you are;
    Albeit knowing the tumult in your soul
    Has quite another cause, my child –

RECHA: What cause,
    Dear father?

NATHAN: Need you ask? Why be so bashful?
    Whatever stirs within you's natural
    And innocent. No need for you to fret.
    I'm not the least perturbed but promise me,
    When finally your heart makes known its wishes,
    You'll not conceal them from me.

RECHA   No, indeed!
    I'd shudder at the thought of such deception.

NATHAN: I'll say no more about it. Once for all,
    The matter's settled. Here comes Daya. Well?

DAYA: He's walking still among the palms-trees and
    Will presently come round the wall. There, look!
    He's coming!

RECHA: He seems quite undecided
    Which way to turn: continue or go back?
    Head left or right?

DAYA: No, no, he likes to walk
    Right round the monastery. He's bound to pass us.
    What will you bet me?

RECHA: Very well. You've spoken
    To him. How is he today?

DAYA: As usual.

NATHAN: Just you take care he doesn't see you waiting.
    Stand back a bit or better still, go right
    Indoors.

RECHA: Just one more glance! Oh, drat the hedge!
   It's stolen him from sight!
DAYA: Come, come, your father's
   Absolutely right. If once he sees you,
   He'll as like as not retreat.
RECHA: Confounded hedge!
NATHAN: Now suddenly he's come out from behind it;
   He cannot help but see you where he is.
   Indoors with you!
DAYA: Come quick! I know a window
   From which we can observe them both!
RECHA: You
   do?
(*They both hurry inside.*)

Scene 5

NATHAN first, then the TEMPLAR.

NATHAN: I'm almost shy of meeting this eccentric.
   I find his stubborn virtue quite forbidding.
   How could one human being so embarrass
   A fellow creature? Here he comes! By Heaven!
   A youth in man's guise. But I like his proud
   Demeanour, sturdy gait. It may well be
   The rind tastes bitter but the nut is sweet.
   Wherever did I see the like of him?
   Forgive me, noble Frank…
TEMPLAR: What's that?
NATHAN: Beg
   pardon…
TEMPLAR: What is it, Jew?
NATHAN: I mean, may I make bold
   To speak with you?
TEMPLAR: Can't stop you, can I?
   Only keep it short.
NATHAN: Forgive me! Pray
   Don't hurry past a man with such disdain
   Whose gratitude eternal you have earned.
TEMPLAR: How so? Ah, I can guess, I think. You are –

NATHAN: My name is Nathan, father of the girl
Who thanks to your unselfishness escaped
The fire…
TEMPLAR: If thanks is on your mind, forget it!
That trifling act's already cost me more
In gratitude than I can bear. Moreover,
You owe me nothing. How was I to know
The girl I rescued was your precious daughter?
It is a Templar's duty at all times
To offer aid regardless, when he sees
Help's needed. Anyway, just then I'd tired
Of living and most willingly I seized
The opportunity to risk my life
To save another's, even were it only
That of a Jewish girl.
NATHAN: A noble deed!
Noble – and yet abhorrent? There are times
When modesty, for fear of admiration,
Takes refuge in a semblance of distaste.
If greatness, though, scorns admiration's tribute,
What tribute would it treat with less disdain?
Templar, if you were not a foreigner
And captive, I might not make bold to ask –
But say – command me – in what way can I
Assist you?
TEMPLAR: Me? In no way.
NATHAN: But I am
A rich man.
TEMPLAR: Far as I'm concerned, no Jew's
A better Jew for being rich.
NATHAN: No matter!
Why not, all the same, just make the best
Of what is best about him? Use his wealth!
TEMPLAR: I won't dismiss the notion out of hand;
Not for my cloak's sake. Maybe when it's all
In shreds and tatters, past repair, then I'll
Come back and borrow from you for a new one –
Cloth or cash! No need to look so grim!

You're safe enough! It's not that bad as yet!
See for yourself! It's still just wearable.
One corner only has a nasty patch
Where it got scorched when I was carrying
Your daughter through the flames.

NATHAN: (*Grasps that corner of the cloak and stares at it.*)
How very odd
That such an ugly mark, that such a burn
Bears louder testimony to a man's brave deed
Than his own tongue! I'd like to kiss that spot.
Forgive me, sir, I couldn't help myself.

TEMPLAR: What now?

NATHAN: A tear drop fell on it.

TEMPLAR: No matter!
It's used to drops! (*Aside.*) This Jew will very soon
Start getting on my nerves!

NATHAN: Would you be kind
Enough to let my daughter also see
This cloak of yours?

TEMPLAR: My cloak? What for?

NATHAN: To press her lips to that discoloured patch,
For it would seem that she must wish in vain
To clasp her arms about your knees.

TEMPLAR: Look, Jew –
Nathan's your name, is it? Look, Nathan –
You speak well – a pretty turn of phrase –
I am nonplussed. I must admit that I'd…

NATHAN: Say what you like, disguise yourself at will!
I see through you! You were too kind, too honest
To treat them more politely. There was she,
A girl a prey to her emotions and her envoy,
All eagerness to serve; her father far
From home. You feared for your good name, and saved
Her virtue being tried. For that I thank you.

TEMPLAR: I must admit, you know how Templars ought
To think.

NATHAN: Why only Templars? And why 'ought'?
Merely because the Order's rules command it?

I know how good men think and well I know
That good men can be found in every land.
TEMPLAR: Despite their differences, I trust.
NATHAN: Of
course,
Their colour, garb and build may vary much.
TEMPLAR: Here or there, a little more or less.
NATHAN: It's much the same here as in other lands.
Everywhere, great men need lots of space:
Plant too many of them too close together
And soon they're breaking one another's branches.
But folk of middling stature, like ourselves,
Are plentiful in every place on earth.
The main thing is to bear with one another:
Rough and smooth accepting, warts and all.
A little peak should not presume to think
Itself the equal of some mighty summit.
TEMPLAR: Well said! But do you know who first began
To plague humanity with prejudice?
Which people, Nathan, first presumed to call
Themselves, among us all, the chosen race?
What if, although I do not hate them for it,
I cannot help myself despising them
For being so arrogant? This pride we have
Inherited from them – Christian and Moslem, too –
Each sure the only true God is his own!
You're shocked to hear a Christian Templar say so?
When and where has this pious lunacy –
Thinking one's own God best and so determined
To force this better God on all the world –
Revealed itself more frightfully than here
And now? Unless the scales fall from their eyes
Both here and now... Be blind who will!
Forget I spoke and leave me! (*Moves to go.*)
NATHAN: By no means!
I'll pursue you all the more. Come!
We must, we simply must be friends! You may
Despise my people to your heart's content;

We neither of us, Templar, chose our race!
Are we our people? What does 'people' mean?
Are Jews and Christans rather Jews and Christians
Than human beings? Haven't I found in you
A man of whom it is enough to say
'This is a man!'

TEMPLAR: Yes, Nathan! That, you have!
You have, by God! Your hand! I am ashamed
To have misjudged you even for an instant.

NATHAN: I'm proud you did. Only what's commonplace
Is misjudged seldom.

TEMPLAR: And what's rare is far
From easily forgotten, Nathan. Yes,
We must, we must be friends!

NATHAN: We are already!
My Recha'll be beside herself with joy!
I see the dawning of a happy future
In the distance. You must get to know her.

TEMPLAR: I truly long to do so. Who's that rushing
From your house? Look! Daya, is it not?

NATHAN: It is! She seems upset.

TEMPLAR: I hope that
nothing's
Happened to our Recha!

Scene 6

DAYA hurriedly joins NATHAN and the TEMPLAR.

DAYA: Nathan! Nathan!

NATHAN: Well?

DAYA: Noble Knight, forgive my interrupting –

NATHAN: What is it then?

TEMPLAR: What is it, Daya, speak –

DAYA: The Sultan's sent a messenger to say
He wants to speak with you. Oh, God – the Sultan!

NATHAN: Me? The Sultan? He'll be curious to see
What novelties I've brought back. Just say,

I've little – or nothing at all – unpacked as yet.
DAYA: No, no, it isn't that. He wants to speak
   To you – in person – and without delay!
NATHAN: Then I shall come. That's all now. Off you go!
DAYA: Please don't be angry with me, noble Knight –
   Oh God, we're so distraught! What can the Sultan
   Want with us?
NATHAN: That we shall see. Go, go!

Scene 7

NATHAN and the TEMPLAR.

TEMPLAR: You still don't know him then? I mean,
   In person.
NATHAN: Sultan Saladin? No, not as yet.
   I've neither tried to meet him nor avoid him.
   His reputation spoke so well of him
   That I was happier to believe it than
   To check. Were it not so, in any case,
   His sparing of your life would seem...
TEMPLAR: Indeed,
   To justify report. If I'm alive,
   It's by his act of grace.
NATHAN: Though which to me
   He's granted double – triple – life,
   Transforming our relationship entirely,
   Forging at once a bond between us which
   Ensures that I'm his servitor for ever.
   Now I can hardly wait to learn the first
   Of his commands. I am prepared for all,
   And gladly will inform him you're the reason.
TEMPLAR: I myself have had no chance to thank him,
   However often I have crossed his path.
   So swift was the impression that I made,
   It must have disappeared no less abruptly.
   Who knows if he remembers me at all?
   And yet, he must recall me once at least
   In order to decide my final fate.
   It's not enough that I am still alive –

By his command and *with* his will, exist,
I must anticipate that he will let me know
According to whose will I have to live.
NATHAN: Quite so. Still less, can I afford to fail.
Some word let slip may give me an excuse
To turn the conversation to your case.
I'm sorry, you'll forgive me if I hurry,
But when shall we enjoy your company
At home?
TEMPLAR: As soon as you permit.
NATHAN: You choose!
TEMPLAR: Today?
NATHAN: Why not? But may I know your
name?
TEMPLAR: My name is Curd von Stauffen. Call me Curd!
NATHAN: Von Stauffen? Stauffen? Stauffen?
TEMPLAR: Is
the name
Known to you?
NATHAN: Von Stauffen? I suppose
The clan has many branches...
TEMPLAR: Yes, the bones
Of many forebears here lie mouldering.
My grandfather himself – my father, rather –
But why, may I ask, are you observing me
With such attention?
NATHAN: Nothing. Pray forgive me!
How could I tire of seeing you?
TEMPLAR: Then I'll
Go first. The searcher's eye too frequently
Finds more than he himself had wished to see.
I fear it, Nathan. Let time take its course –
Time and not curiosity acquaintance build.
(*He walks away.*)
NATHAN: (*Staring after him in astonishment.*)
He said 'The searcher's eye too frequently
Finds more than he himself had wished to see.'
Astonishing! It really is as though

He'd read my inmost thoughts! It must be so...
That such a thing could happen to myself:
Same build as Wolf, his walk, and voice the same,
The selfsame trick of tossing back his head!
The way Wolf bore his sword and stroked his brow,
As though to shield his fiery gaze from sight –
Amazing how such pictures deeply etched
Will slumber in the mind for years until
Awakened by a word, a sound – Von Stauffen!
Of course! Who else, but Filnek and Von Stauffen?
I'll find out more about all this – and soon!
But first, to Saladin! No, isn't that
Our Daya lurking still? Daya, come here!

Scene 8

DAYA and NATHAN.

NATHAN: What's this? The pair of you are now intent
   On learning something quite apart from what
   The Sultan wants me for.
DAYA: You wouldn't blame her?
   Your conversation with him had become
   More confidential when the Sultan's envoy
   Drove us from the window.
NATHAN: You just tell her
   That any moment now she may expect
   A visit from the Templar.
DAYA: True?
NATHAN: Can I
   Rely on you? Daya, be on your guard,
   I beg of you; have nothing to repent!
   Your own good conscience should ensure it, but
   Take care; in no way jeopardise my plan.
   Tell stories and ask questions modestly
   And with restraint...
DAYA: That you remember that
   Just now! I'm going. You, too, better go.

I think the Sultan's second messenger
Is coming now: your Dervish friend, Al Hafi!
(*Exit DAYA.*)

Scene 9

NATHAN and AL HAFI.

AL HAFI: Ha! I was about to call on you again!
NATHAN: Is it that urgent? What does he want me for?
AL HAFI: Who?
NATHAN: Why, Saladin! I'm on my way.
AL HAFI: To whom? To Saladin?
NATHAN: Did he not send you?
AL HAFI: Me? No. Has he sent for you already?
NATHAN: Indeed, he has.
AL HAFI: Then that's the way of it.
NATHAN: What's that supposed to mean?
AL HAFI: It's not
    my fault.
    God knows, I'm not to blame! As if I didn't
    Lie my head off for you to prevent it!
NATHAN: Prevent what? Out with it!
AL HAFI: He's making
    you
    His Treasurer. You have my sympathy.
    But I'll not wait around to see it happen!
    I'm going now – at once – I've told you where
    And you already know the route. If there
    Is anything that I can do for you
    Along the way, I'm at your service, though
    It better not weigh more than bare-back tramp
    Can haul!
NATHAN: Al Hafi, have you gone quite mad?
    Collect your wits! All this is news to me!
    What do you mean?
AL HAFI: You've got it with you now –
    The purse, that is?
NATHAN: What purse?

AL HAFI: The money you're
   About to lend to Sultan Saladin!

NATHAN: That's all that worries you?

AL HAFI: Am I supposed
   To stand and watch him drain you day by day –
   Bleed you white from top to toe? Stand by
   And watch while spendthrift generosity
   From granaries that once were ever full,
   Borrows and borrows, borrows till at last,
   Even the poorest mice who've always lived there
   Starve to death! Nathan, you don't imagine –
   Gorging your cash – he'll swallow your advice?
   Him take advice! Did ever Saladin
   Heed an advisor? Listen while I tell you
   What happened when I called on him just now.

NATHAN: What, then?

AL HAFI: He'd just been playing chess
   Against his sister, Sittah, who's not bad.
   The game that Saladin believed he'd lost
   Was still upon the board when I arrived.
   I saw at once that Saladin resigned
   When still the game was very far from
   Lost.

NATHAN: A nice discovery for you!

AL HAFI: He'd only got to move his King to pawn
   To check her. I just wish that I could show
   You how it was!

NATHAN: Oh, I believe you, Hafi!

AL HAFI: That would have freed his rook and finished her.
   All of this I drew to his attention.
   Think of that!

NATHAN: He didn't share your view?

AL HAFI: He wouldn't listen, tossed the game aside,
   Scattering the chess-men in contempt.

NATHAN: Can it be so?

AL HAFI: He said he wished for once
   To be check-mated, if you please! I ask you!
   Wished! You call that playing?

NATHAN: Hardly that!
  Not playing chess, but playing with it.
AL HAFI: Waste
  Of time and effort!
NATHAN: Money squandered, too!
  That's the least of it! What's worse by far:
  Not listening to you, scorning your advice
  On such a vital matter, that's the sin!
  The failure to admire your eagle-eye
  Cries out for retribution, does it not?
AL HAFI: Come, come! I only mentioned it to show you
  What a stubborn man the Sultan is.
  In short, I cannot stand him any longer!
  He has me running round these dirty Moors
  Trying to find one who will lend him cash.
  That I, who never begged a crust to feed
  Myself, should have to borrow for another.
  For borrowing cash is much the same as begging,
  And lending cash for interest scarcely more
  Than outright theft. Among my fellow Parsees
  On the Ganges, I shall have no need of either,
  Nor need I be the tool of any man.
  Beside the Ganges, men are simply men.
  You are the only person here who's worthy
  To live by the Ganges! Won't you come with me?
  Leave him high and dry with all his loot –
  That's all he cares about! He'd kill you
  Slowly and at least thereby cut short
  Your torment. Better let me find a robe
  For you and come away!
NATHAN: I thought that might
  Well prove our last resort. But wait, Al Hafi,
  First, I must reflect –
AL HAFI: Reflect, you say?
  No call for leisurely reflexion –
NATHAN: Only
  Till I return from Saladin; until
  I first take leave…

AL HAFI: He who reflects already
Seeks for reasons why he can't. He who's
Unable to decide at once to live
His own life, lives for ever slave to others.
Do as you see fit! I wish you well.
You've chosen your way and I've chosen mine.
NATHAN: Before you go, Al Hafi, don't you need
To settle your accounts?
AL HAFI: You must be joking!
The cash in hand's not worth a hill of beans;
My debts? You'll guarantee them – you or Sittah!
Farewell!
(*Exit AL HAFI.*)
NATHAN: (*Watching him leave.*)
    Me guarantee? What's one to make
Of him? Mad, kind or noble? It's a fact –
None but the outright beggar's truly King!
(*Exit NATHAN in opposite direction.*)

End of Act Two.

ACT THREE

Scene 1

Nathan's house.

RECHA and DAYA.

RECHA: Daya, what was the phrase my father used –
    I could 'expect the Templar any moment...'
    I thought that meant he'd lose no time in coming.
    How many moments though have passed already?
    But moments past aren't worth considering;
    From now on, I will live and live alone
    In every future moment as it comes –
    And one of them will surely bring him here!

DAYA: Oh, that accursed message from the Sultan!
    Had it not been for that, Nathan could well
    Have brought him home at once.

RECHA: But when it
    comes –
    The moment he arrives – and my most ardent
    Wish is granted me, what then?

DAYA: What then?
    Then, I would hope the warmest of my wishes
    Would also be fulfilled.

RECHA: But what shall take
    Its place in my poor heart, so long unused
    To life without one dominant desire?
    Nothing? I'm terrified!

DAYA: Why so? My wish
    Will fill the vacant space – my wish
    To see you live in Europe and to know
    That you're in worthy hands and safely lodged.

RECHA: You're wrong. What makes that wish appeal to you
    Ensures it can't be mine. Your homeland draws you;
    Should not mine attract me equally?

Do you suppose the image of your people,
Still vivid in your mind, is stronger than
My sense of those folk visible to me –
I touch and hear around me all day long –
My people!
DAYA: You may argue all you like.
But heaven's ways, my dear, are heaven's ways.
What if it were your Templar Knight himself
Through whom his God, the God for whom he fights,
Desired that you be taken to that land
And people you were born to live among?
RECHA: Dear Daya, now what nonsense are you talking?
You have the strangest notions, I must say!
'*His* God,' you said, 'the God for whom he fights'?
To whom does God belong? What sort of God
Would be man's chattel or need fighting for?
Moreover, how can any person tell
The spot on earth in which he's meant to live
Unless it be the land in which he's born?
If father were to hear you say such things!
What has he done to you that you insist
On trying to persuade me I'll be happy
As far away as possible from him?
Does he deserve that you should try to mix
The seeds of purest reason sown in my mind
By him, with the weeds and flowers of your land?
The fact is, Daya dear, he does not want
To see your flowers blooming in my soil!
And I myself, I must say, feel my earth –
However prettily you plant it – quite
Debilitated, drained by your bright flowers.
The bitter-sweet aroma of their scent
Numbs my wits; my head spins! As for you,
Your brain is used to it. I don't condemn
Your stouter nerves accustomed to the strain.
It's simply not for me. Quite recently.
You and your angels all but made a fool
Of me: I'm blushing still in front of father!

Piffle!

DAYA: As though in this house – nowhere else –
Is wisdom heard! You call it piffle! Piffle!
If only I were free to speak!

RECHA: What's stopping you?
Was I not all ears, when you were pleased
To tell me stirring tales about the heroes
Of your religion? Did I ever fail
To voice my admiration of their deeds?
Or copiously weep to hear their pains?
Admittedly their faith did not strike me
As what was most heroic in their nature.
Far more consoling, to my mind, the doctrine
That submission to God's will does not at all
Depend on what we fancy Him to be!
Many a time my father said so, Daya,
And you repeatedly agreed with him.
So why are you, alone, now trying to undo
What you and he together have constructed?
Dear Daya, is this any conversation
With which to greet the friend that
We're expecting? For me, perhaps it is;
At all costs, I must know whether he, too…
Whisht, Daya! Someone at the door, I think!
It could be him! Hush, listen!

Scene 2

*RECHA, DAYA and the TEMPLAR, for whom someone outside
has opened the gate with the words: 'Enter, sir!'*

RECHA: (*Sudden start, controls herself and prepares to fall at his
feet.*) He's here! My rescuer!

TEMPLAR: Just what I
hoped
I might avoid. I took my time, yet –

RECHA: Here,
At the feet of this proud man, I wish
God alone to thank – and not the man.

He no more wishes to be thanked than does
The water-bucket which so busily
Helped douse the flames, unmindful of us both,
Letting itself be emptied and refilled
Repeatedly. Likewise, this man who let
Himself be somehow thrust into the blaze.
I merely fell by chance into his arms
And, like a spark adhering to his cloak,
Remained there resting safe in his embrace,
Till something, Lord alone knows what it was,
Expelled us both from the inferno. What
Need for thanks? In Europe, wine makes men
Perform far doughtier deeds. But Templar Knights
Are duty-bound to act in such a way –
Much as the best of trained retrievers snatch
A crippled bird from fire no less than flood.

TEMPLAR: (*Who has observed her throughout with astonishment
and uneasiness.*)
O Daya! If in moments of distress
And spleen, my temper served you ill, why did
You have to quote to her each foolish word
And phrase which then my tongue let slip?
That was too cruel a vengeance to exact!
I only hope, from now on, you'll be able
To present me to her in a better light.

DAYA: Sir Knight, I do not think those little barbs
Of yours, which pricked her heart, have done you any
Lasting damage there.

RECHA: You suffered grief,
You say, yet hugged your grief so greedily,
While spendthrift with your life?

TEMPLAR: My dear good
child!
Oh, how my heart is torn between the ear
And eye! This cannot be the selfsame girl
I rescued from the fire! Who could have known
This girl and *not* have rescued her? Who would
Have waited till I did? True, fear distorts.

113

(*A pause during which TEMPLAR appears lost in
contemplation of RECHA.*)

RECHA: *You* look the same to me; you haven't changed!
  (*Pause while she stares at him, then continues speaking, in
  order to interrupt his contemplation.*)
  Sir Knight, do tell us where you've been so long?
  I might well ask if you are with us now?

TEMPLAR: I am where, possibly, I should not be.

RECHA: Where were you? Somewhere else perhaps you think
  You'd better not have been? Sounds bad to me.

TEMPLAR: I was on – what's that mountain called? Ah, yes –
  Mount Sinai.

RECHA: It's beautiful, up there!
  Now, maybe you can tell me for a fact
  Whether it's true...

TEMPLAR: What's true? No doubt you mean
  Whether the spot can still be seen where Moses
  Stood before God when...

RECHA: No, that isn't it!
  Wherever he was standing, he faced God;
  Besides, I know all that. But you perhaps
  Can tell me what I really want to learn:
  They say it's far more difficult to climb
  That mountain than it is to scramble down.
  Can that be so? Because, to judge by those
  I've climbed, the opposite is true.
  Come, Knight – what's wrong? Why turn away?
  Can't bear to face me?

TEMPLAR: I just want to hear you.

RECHA: I suppose you don't want me to see that
  My simplicity has made you smile –
  Since I had nothing more intelligent
  To ask about this holiest of mountains.
  Am I not right, good Templar?

TEMPLAR: In that case,
  I must look once more into your eyes.
  Why cast them down, your smile so soon suppress?
  In gestures, dubious gestures must I read
  What I could hear, what you so audibly
  Were telling me – now hushed? Ah, Recha, Recha!

As he rightly said: 'First get to know her!'

RECHA: Who said that? About whom? Who was it?

TEMPLAR: 'First get to know her!' were your father's words –
To me, about yourself.

DAYA: My very words!
Did I not say the same?

TEMPLAR: Where is he, then?
Where is your father? With the Sultan still?

RECHA: No doubt they'd plenty to discuss.

TEMPLAR: (*Anxiously.*) Still there?
Head like a sieve! He must have left the Palace:
He'll be waiting for me by the cloister.
I think that's what we both agreed. Forgive me!
I'll go and fetch him...

DAYA: Please leave that to me.
You stay, Sir Knight. I'll bring him back at once.

TEMPLAR: No, no, he'll be expecting me, not you!
Besides, who knows, he could quite easily –
The Sultan could – you don't know Saladin.
He could quite easily run into trouble.
Believe me, there could very well be danger
Unless I go...

RECHA: Danger, you say? What danger?

TEMPLAR: Danger for me, for you, for him, should I
Delay – no time to lose!
(*Exit TEMPLAR.*)

Scene 3

RECHA and DAYA.

RECHA: What is it, Daya?
Why such haste! Whatever drove him out?
What came over him?

DAYA: Don't worry, let him go.
It may be no bad sign.

RECHA: A sign of what?

DAYA: A sign that something's going on inside:
Something is boiling, but must not boil over.

Let him go. The rest is up to you!

RECHA: What is? I'm lost. You're making no more sense
Than he does.

DAYA: You will very soon be able
To pay him back for worrying you so much.
But do not be too harsh, nor over-vengeful.

RECHA: No doubt you've some idea of what you mean.

DAYA: Don't tell me that you now feel quite at ease!

RECHA: I do, indeed I am…

DAYA: At least, admit
You're pleased to see him anxious for a change,
And thanks to that, can now yourself enjoy
Some peace of mind.

RECHA: If so, unconsciously!
The most I would allow to you is that
I'm quite surprised, myself, how suddenly
My heart – so long in turmoil – has regained
Its peace. By sight and sound of him – his tone –
I've been –

DAYA: Already satisfied?

RECHA: I won't say that.
No, truth to tell, I'm far from satisfied.

DAYA: The hunger-pangs just eased?

RECHA: Well, yes
– perhaps –
Yes, if you will.

DAYA: Not my concern.

RECHA: To me,
He'll always be most dear and dearer still
Than life itself, that's even should my pulse
No longer race at mention of his name,
My heart, at very thought of him, no longer
Faster and more strongly beat! Enough!!
Dear Daya, quick! Back to that window which
Looks out towards the palms.

DAYA: So they're not quite
Appeased, those hunger pangs?

RECHA: I want to see
The palms again, not only him beneath them.

DAYA: I'd say this momentary chill is but

The prelude to another bout of fever.
RECHA: What chill? I'm far from cold and more than pleased
To see what's to be seen, with mind at rest.

Scene 4

An audience hall in Saladin's palace.

SALADIN and SITTAH.

SALADIN: (*Towards the door, as he enters.*)
Bring in the Jew as soon as he arrives!
He seems in no great hurry to appear.
SITTAH: Most likely he was out. It's taking time
To find him.
SALADIN: Sister! Sister!
SITTAH: You're behaving
As though about to fight a duel.
SALADIN: A duel
With weapons I've not learnt to handle.
I must dissemble and intimidate,
Lay snares and tip-toe gently on thin ice.
Things I could never do, for where could I
Such skills acquire? Moreover, what's the point?
To fish for money – money! Just to scare
The ducats from a Jew with whom I am
Reduced to paltry ruses finally
In order to obtain the least of trifles!
SITTAH: A trifle scorned too harshly, brother,
Surely takes revenge.
SALADIN: Alas, that's true!
But should this Jew turn out to be the good
And reasonable man the Dervish first
Described to you, what then?
SITTAH: What then?
That needn't worry us! The trap befits
Only the miserly, cautious, timid Jew
And not the good, wise man. For he's already
Ours and needs no snare. The pleasure you'll

117

Take in hearing such a man defend
His case, with what bold show of strength he'll snap
The rope or, with deft cunning wriggle through
The net – all that, you'll relish thoroughly!

SALADIN: Indeed I shall; you're right and I'm already
Looking forward to it.

SITTAH: So, why worry?
What else is there for you to fret about?
He's one of a throng – a Jew like any other!
Would you not feel ashamed if you appeared
To him as he already views all men?
Indeed, the better he perceives a man to be,
The more a Jew regards him as a fool.

SALADIN: In that case, what you're saying is that I
Must act the villain lest a villain should
Think ill of me?

SITTAH: True, if it's villainy
To make good use of what occasion offers.

SALADIN: Did ever woman's head conceive a ploy
She could not cunningly commend?

SITTAH: How so?

SALADIN: I need but take this fine-spun scheme of yours
In my coarse hands for it to fall apart.
Its execution needs the wit and skill
Of its conceiver. But I'll do my best
To dance as you direct, albeit it rather
Worse than better.

SITTAH: Have self-confidence!
I shall support you, should you so desire.
Men like you assure us all too often,
The sword alone – and nothing but the sword –
Has made them what they are. No doubt the lion,
When he goes out hunting with the fox,
May scorn the fox himself, but not his cunning!

SALADIN: Women are all too keen to drag men down
To their own level, sister! Off you go!
I think I've got my lesson off by heart.

SITTAH: What? Should I leave?

SALADIN: You didn't mean to stay?

SITTAH: If not beside you, very close at hand –
In that adjoining room perhaps?

SALADIN: To eavesdrop?
No, not even that, I must insist.
Be off! The curtain's rustling. He is here!
Don't wait about. Just go! I'll deal with this.
(*While she leaves by one door, NATHAN enters by the
other. SALADIN now seated.*)

Scene 5

SALADIN and NATHAN.

SALADIN: Come closer, Jew! Still closer! Here, beside me!
Do not fear!

NATHAN: Fear's for your foes to feel!

SALADIN: Nathan you call yourself?

NATHAN: Yes.

SALADIN: Nathan
the Wise?

NATHAN: No.

SALADIN: Well, if you don't, the people do!

NATHAN: The people – possibly.

SALADIN: You don't
suggest
I'd treat the people's verdict with contempt?
I've long desired to meet the man they call
The Wise.

NATHAN: What if they merely dub him so
In mockery? If wise, in people's eyes,
Means simply clever – clever being he
Who always knows what's in his interest?

SALADIN: His own true interest, you mean to say?

NATHAN: If so, the most self-interested man
Would clearly be the cleverest of all
And wise and clever both would mean the same.

SALADIN: I hear you proving what you would deny.
What's best for man, the people do not know,

But you do. You, at least, have tried to learn;
You've thought about it deeply. That alone
Denotes the wise man...
NATHAN: Each believes himself
To be.
SALADIN: Enough of all this modesty!
It cloys to hear too much of it when one
Expects to hear the cold, dry voice of reason.
(*He jumps up.*)
Let's now get down to business! But let's talk
Openly, Jew! Plain-speaking, d'ye hear?
NATHAN: Sultan, I assure you that I wish
To serve you in such way as to be worthy
Of your continued patronage in future.
SALADIN: Serve? How?
NATHAN: You, Sire, shall receive the very
best
Of all I can provide and you shall have it
At the lowest price!
SALADIN: What can you mean?
Surely not your wares! My sister haggles –
(*Aside.*) Teach her to eavesdrop, if she's still about!
(*Aloud.*) I don't have anything to do with merchants.
NATHAN: Then, doubtless, you will wish to hear from me
Whether on my travels I have seen
Or met your enemies, now said to be
Once more astir? To tell the honest truth –
SALADIN: That wasn't what I hoped to hear from you.
About such things, I know enough already –
All I need to know. In short –
NATHAN: Command me!
SALADIN: I want your views on quite another topic.
Entirely different. Since you are so wise,
Be good enough to tell me, if you would,
Which religion or what rule for living
Do you find most illuminating?
NATHAN: Sultan,
I'm a Jew.

SALADIN: And I'm a Moslem. Twixt us two,
There's Christianity. And of these three,
But one alone can possibly be true.
A man like you does not just stay where he's
Been planted by the accident of birth,
Or, if he does, deciding it is best,
His choice is based on judgement and conviction.
That being so, I'm asking you to share
With me the strength of your conviction.
Tell me the reasons which, myself, I've not
Had time to study. Tell me – in confidence,
Of course – the reasons governing your choice,
That I may make it mine. What? You're amazed?
You try to size me up? If I should be
The only Sultan plagued by such a whim,
It's not, I think, unworthy of a Sultan.
Don't you agree with me? Then speak your mind,
Or do you want a moment to reflect?
I grant it you. (*Aside.*) Has she been listening?
I'd like to ask her how she thinks I'm doing.
(*Aloud.*) Think it over, but don't take too long.
Be quick! I'm coming back!
(*He goes into the adjoining room to which SITTAH has withdrawn.*)

Scene 6

NATHAN alone.

NATHAN: It's very strange!
Where do I stand? And what's the Sultan after?
I thought he wanted cash; he asks for truth!
Demanding it in such a bare-faced way –
As though the truth itself were just a coin –
Albeit of a bygone age – that must be weighed.
It could be that! But truth is no fresh coin,
Stamped with a ruler's face, whose value
Can be reckoned. Can the truth be swept
Into man's head, like coins into a bag?

Which of us is the Jew, then? He or I
Yet, why should he not in truth demand the truth?
It seems too petty to suspect he's using truth
To trap me... But who knows what great men
Judge too petty? True, he broke the door down,
So to speak. Should not a friend approaching
Knock first, then listen? I must tread with care.
But how? Won't do to be too strict a Jew...
Though not behaving like a Jew at all, still less!
For were I not a Jew, he might well ask:
Why not be Moslem, then? I think I've got it!
As children are fobbed off with fairy-tales,
So men can be! He's coming back. Well, let him!

Scene 7

SALADIN and NATHAN.

SALADIN: (*Aside.*) The field is clear. (*Aloud.*) I've not
                                                returned too
    soon
    For you, I hope? I take it you have reached
    The limit of your cogitations ? Good!
    Speak. We can't be overheard.
NATHAN: Would all the world
    Could hear us parley!
SALADIN: Are you then so sure
    Of your contention? That's what I call wise:
    Not to conceal the truth and be prepared
    To stake your all upon it! Life and limb.
    Every stick you own, each drop of blood!
NATHAN: Why, yes, if need be and it serves a purpose.
SALADIN: From now on, may I hope to bear at least
    One of my titles worthily. To wit:
    Reformer of the world and of the Law.
NATHAN: A comely title, that! But if I may –
    Before unburdening my thoughts to you –
    Will you permit me to relate a story?
SALADIN: Why not? I've always lent a willing ear

To stories if well told.

NATHAN: I wouldn't say
That I'm the best of story-tellers.

SALADIN: Come!
There you go again, so proudly modest –
Just set about your tale, I want to hear it!

NATHAN: Once, somewhere in the East, there lived a man
Possessor of a ring of priceless worth,
The gift of one much-loved. The stone was opal,
Whose facets flashed a hundred varied hues –
A stone imbued with the mysterious power
Of rendering those who wore it in good faith,
Pleasing in both the sight of God and man.
No wonder that its owner in the East
Could never bear to take it off his finger
And furthermore took measures to ensure
The ring would never leave his family.
Thus he bequeathed it to his favourite son
And stipulated that he, too, must leave it
To whichever son he loved the best,
Who then by virtue, not of birth but of the ring,
Became the family head with title Count.
You follow, Sultan?

SALADIN: Yes, of course. Go on!

NATHAN: And so the ring was passed from son to son,
Until it reached a father who had three,
Each of whom was equally devoted,
The father, loving each one equally
Was quite unable to forgo the habit.
From time to time, however, it befell
That one or other of them, or the third,
Would seem to him most worthy, when but one
Was with him and no need to share his heart.
And so to each in turn, from pious weakness,
The father promised all three sons the ring.
While still he lived, there wasn't any problem.
But when he came to die, he was perplexed.
He couldn't bear the thought of disappointing

Two of the three relying on his word.
He therefore sent in secret for a craftsman
And bade him make two rings which matched the first;
Nor cost nor trouble must he spare until
The three rings were alike in every detail.
The craftsman did so. When the rings were brought,
The father himself could not tell true from false.
In glad relief, he called each son in turn –
To each his blessing gave, to each a ring –
Then died in peace. You're listening, are you, Sultan?

SALADIN: *(Has turned away from him, perplexed.)*
 Yes, of course! But hurry! Is this fable
 Nearly ended?

NATHAN: I have finished, Sire.
 The rest of it is easy to predict.
 No sooner was the father dead than each
 Of his three sons with ring in hand proclaimed
 Himself the family head with title Count.
 Investigations, quarrels and complaints
 Ensued. In vain. For nobody could prove
 Which ring was genuine.
 (After a pause during which he awaits for the Sultan to reply.)
        No more than we
 Today can prove which faith is true.

SALADIN: How so?
 Is that your answer to my question?

NATHAN: Pray
 Forgive me, if I cannot trust myself
 To choose between those rings the father made
 So that all three should be identical.

SALADIN: The rings! Don't trifle with me, Nathan!
 I'd have thought the three religions that
 I mentioned very simple to define –
 Not least by way of clothing, food and drink!

NATHAN: But not as far as origin's concerned!
 For are not all three based on history –
 Written or conveyed by word of mouth?

And history must assuredly be taken
On trust and faith alone, don't you agree?
Whose faith and trust, then, do we doubt the least?
Our own, of course; those of our kith and kin!
Of those who, from our childhood, have bestowed
Proofs of their love for us? Deceiving never,
Save where they thought deception beneficial.
How can I trust my forebears less than you
Trust yours? And vice versa. How can I demand
That you accuse your ancestors of lying
In order not to contradict my own?
And vice versa. Christians likewise, surely?

SALADIN: (*Aside.*) By the living God, the man is right!
　　He's silenced me!

NATHAN:　　　　　　Reverting to the ring,
　　As I've just said, the three sons went to law
　　And each of them assured the judge on oath
　　That he'd received the ring directly from
　　His father's hand – which was indeed the truth –
　　The father having promised each long since
　　That one day he'd enjoy the privilege
　　Attaching to the ring – quite true, again.
　　Each son insisted that his father never would
　　Have played him false and rather than suspect
　　A parent so devoted, each – while wishing
　　Only to believe the best – concluded
　　Sadly that his brothers must have lied.
　　Each was certain he could prove the others
　　Traitors and exact his just revenge.

SALADIN: But what about the judge? I'd like to hear
　　What words you'll put into his mouth! Go on!

NATHAN: The judge said, if you can't produce your father
　　As a witness, I'll dismiss the case.
　　It's not my job as judge to solve a riddle.
　　Or did you think of waiting here until
　　The true ring is prepared to testify?
　　Just a moment! I believe the ring
　　In question has the magic power to make

Its owner pleasing both to God and man.
That should decide it! If the rings are false
They'll clearly not possess that power. Now, whom
Do two of you love best? Speak up! You can't?
So do the rings work only inwardly?
It seems each only loves himself the best.
All three of you deceivers are deceived!
All three rings are fakes. Your father must
Have lost the true ring and to hide his loss
Had three more made.

SALADIN: That's marvellous! Go on!

NATHAN: So, said the judge, if you don't wish to hear
From me advice, instead of verdict, you may go!
But my advice is: leave things as they are.
You've each of you received his father's ring,
So let each one continue to believe
His own is genuine. Who knows, perhaps
Your father could no longer bear the strain
Of having *one* ring tyrannise his heirs,
And since he loved three sons, all equally,
Refused to favour one, depriving two.
Let each of you now seek to emulate
That pure affection, free from prejudice.
Let each of you compete to demonstrate
The magic virtue vested in his ring
And help that power to grow with gentleness,
With heartfelt tolerance, with charity
And deep submission to the will of God!
Then, should the magic opal's power one day
Imbue your children's children's children,
I invite them – thousands of years from now –
To stand before this judgement seat, whereon
Will sit and speak a wiser man than I.
Now go! said the modest judge.

SALADIN: Oh, God is great!

NATHAN: If, Saladin, you feel yourself to be
That promised, wiser man…

SALADIN: (*Rushing towards him and seizing his hand which he
continues holding throughout.*) I'm dust! I'm nothing!
Lord God!

NATHAN: What is it, Saladin?
SALADIN: Oh, Nathan,
  Nathan! Your judge's many thousand years
  Have still to run. His judgement seat's not mine!
  Go, Nathan, go! But always be my friend!
NATHAN: Has Saladin no further word to say?
SALADIN: Nothing.
NATHAN: Nothing?
SALADIN: Not a word – but, why?
NATHAN: I would have liked the chance to beg a favour.
SALADIN: To beg a favour? You have but to speak.
NATHAN: I'm just back from a very lengthy journey,
  Collecting long-outstanding debts, which means
  I've almost too much cash in hand. Now that
  The times give rise to some concern, I hardly
  Know where best to store it and since war
  Seems imminent and extra funds required,
  I wondered whether possibly you might
  Not be in need?
SALADIN: (*Looking him hard in the eye.*)
                    I shall not ask you, Nathan,
  Whether Al Hafi called on you already;
  Nor yet inquire if some suspicion prompted
  You to volunteer…
NATHAN: You say suspicion?
SALADIN: I deserve it. Pardon me. What use pretending?
  I must confess to you that I was on the point
  Of –
NATHAN: Not suggesting it yourself?
SALADIN: I was.
NATHAN: Then this would help us both. I'd send you all
  My ready cash, were it not for the Templar –
  Known to you, I think – to whom I am indebted
  And must pay a certain sum.
SALADIN: A Templar Knight?
  You're not proposing also to support
  My bitterest enemies with your wealth, I trust?
NATHAN: I'm speaking only of the single Templar Knight
  Whose life you spared…
SALADIN: Now, you've reminded me,

127

I'd quite forgotten that young Templar. What,
You already know him? Where's he gone?

NATHAN: But you don't know how great the consequence
To me and mine, through him, of your compassion:
He bravely hazarded his new-found life
By rescuing my daughter from a fire.

SALADIN: He did, did he? He looked that kind of man.
My brother would have done the same, I swear.
They were so much alike! Is he still here?
Then bring him to me! I have told my sister
Tales of this brother whom she never knew;
I'd like to let her see his living image!
Go fetch him!

NATHAN: (*Letting go of SALADIN's hand.*)
                    On the instant! For the rest,
Our bargain stands. (*Exit NATHAN.*)

SALADIN: Why didn't I let my sister
Stay and eavesdrop? I must find her quickly!
So much to tell, I won't know where to start!
(*Exit SALADIN in opposite direction.*)

Scene 8

*The TEMPLAR is waiting for NATHAN among the palm-trees
near the monastery.*

TEMPLAR: (*Striding to and fro, struggling with himself, before
bursting out.*) Here let the weary scapegoat pause awhile!
Enough! I do not wish to know precisely
What's happening inside me, nor to sense,
Ahead of time, what may. It's clear, I fled
In vain; no point at all in trying to escape.
Yet there was nothing else I could have done!
Now I must face the future, come what may.
Fate struck too suddenly for me to dodge
The blow I'd been evading for so long:
The sight of her I was so loath to see,
The sight and the decision never more
To let her from my sight. I say decision,

But decision would imply a conscious act;
I merely suffered, passive – saw and felt
Enmeshed in her and woven in her being,
All at once! To live apart from her
Is now unthinkable and would be death –
Here and wherever we exist beyond!
If that is love, then, Templar – you're in love!
A Christian loves a Jewish girl, that's all.
What matter? In the Promised Land, I've rid
Myself of many a prejudice, and so,
For me, 'twill always be the Promised Land.
What of my Order? As a Templar, I
Am dead – as good as slain at once by him
Who captured me. The head that Saladin
Gave back to me was not my old one but
A new head, purged of inculcated views
And fetter-free – a better head, it is,
More suited to my father's kind of Heaven.
With this new head I have begun to think
As father must have done when he was here,
Unless the tales about him I've heard tell
Were lies. Tales? But highly credible
And never more so to my ears than now,
As I risk stumbling where my father fell.
Fell? I'd sooner fall with men than stand
With children. His example guarantees
Me his approval. Whose approval else
Concerns me – Nathan's? There, encouragement –
Approval, too – are sure. How fine a Jew!
And how he revels in his Jewishness!
He's coming, walking quickly, radiant.
How else does anyone leave Saladin?
Hey, Nathan, hey!

Scene 9

NATHAN and TEMPLAR.

NATHAN: It's you, is it?

TEMPLAR: You spent
    A long time with the Sultan, didn't you?
NATHAN: Not so long. I was delayed as I set out
    And got there late. The Sultan's rightly famed.
    The fame is but a shadow of the fact!
    But first of all, just let me tell you quickly –
TEMPLAR: What?
NATHAN: The Sultan wants to speak to you!
    He bids you to the Palace without fail.
    But first, come home with me. There's something I
    Must do for him at once. Together then
    We'll go to Saladin.
TEMPLAR: Nathan, I'd sooner not
    Enter your house again...
NATHAN: So you've been in
    Already, have you? Did you speak to her?
    Out with it, my friend! How did you like
    My Recha?
TEMPLAR: She... She's quite beyond compare!
    But, see her even once again...I cannot –
    Never! Unless you promise here and now,
    That I'll be able to behold her always
    And for ever!
NATHAN: What am I to make
    Of what you say?
TEMPLAR: (*After a short pause, embraces him.*)
    My father!
NATHAN: Come, young man!
TEMPLAR: (*Retreating just as speedily.*) Not
    son?
    I beg you, Nathan!
NATHAN: But my dear young man!
TEMPLAR: Not son? I beg you, Nathan! I entreat of you
    By nature's foremost bonds, do not reject
    Them! Do not opt for fetters later but
    Content yourself with being the man you are!
    Don't thrust me from you!
NATHAN: Ah, dear friend!

TEMPLAR:
And son?
Not son? Still not? Though gratitude has smoothed
Love's pathway to your daughter's eager heart?
Not even when two souls await your sign
To merge as one? Oh, Nathan, you are silent...
NATHAN: You've taken me completely by surprise!
TEMPLAR: Surprise? How could I have surprised you, Nathan,
With your own thoughts? Or is it that you do
Not recognise them on my lips? Surprise!
NATHAN: First, young friend, I need to know what kind
Of Stauffen your late father was.
TEMPLAR: You what!
At such a moment, Nathan, all you feel
Is curiosity?
NATHAN: The point is, I
Once knew a Stauffen long ago whose name
Was Conrad.
TEMPLAR: What if that *was* my father's name?
NATHAN: A fact?
TEMPLAR: I, also, bear my father's name –
For Curd is Conrad.
NATHAN: Can't have been your father!
My Conrad – like yourself, a Templar Knight –
Was never married.
TEMPLAR: So?
NATHAN: How?
TEMPLAR: Notwithstanding,
He could have been my father...
NATHAN: You are joking.
TEMPLAR: You're being a shade particular. Why not
A love-child or a bastard, as they say.
The breed is not to be despised. But come,
If you'll spare me ancestral inquisition,
I'll do the same for you. Not that I've
The slightest doubt about *your* family tree.
No, God forbid! There's not a leaf astray
Right up to Abraham! The same thereafter.
That, I know and I can swear it's so.

NATHAN: You're growing bitter! But do I deserve it?
    I cast no slur on you. I only wanted
    You to voice what I had thought to see.
    And that was all.
TEMPLAR: You're certain that was all?
    Forgive me, then…
NATHAN: Come on, let's go –
TEMPLAR: Where
    to?
    No, not your house again! Not that! I can't!
    Too hot in there! I'll wait for you. You go!
    If I see her once more, then I'll be sure
    Of seeing her more often. But if not –
    Then I've already seen far, far too much
    Of her…
NATHAN: I'll be as quick as possible.

Scene 10

TEMPLAR, shortly joined by DAYA.

TEMPLAR: More than enough! The human brain can hold
    A limitless amount and yet at times
    It suddenly feels full! An extra trifle –
    And it's suddenly packed tight. No room!
    Regardless of what's filling it already.
    Patience, though! The spirit sets to work
    And kneads the steamy mix until its space
    And light and order are restored. Am I
    In love for the first time? Or was what I thought
    Most surely love, not true love after all?
    Is real love what I'm feeling now?
DAYA: (*Creeping in from the side.*) Sir Knight!
TEMPLAR: Who's calling? Oh, it's Daya…
DAYA: Yes, I crept
    Right past him. But where you are standing
    He can see us both. Step back a bit –
    Closer to me – and hide behind this tree.
TEMPLAR: What is it? Why the secrecy? What's wrong?

DAYA: It is in fact a secret which now brings
    Me here – to be precise, a pair of secrets:
    One, known only to myself, the second
    Known to you alone. Shall we exchange?
    If you'll confide to me your secret, I'll
    Make known my own to you.
TEMPLAR: With pleasure!
    But tell me first what you consider mine
    And doubtless that will clarify your own.
    You start!
DAYA: No, that won't do, Sir Knight! Yours first,
    Then mine! My secret won't be any use
    To you unless I hear yours first. Be quick!
    For if I have to drag yours out of you,
    You'll have confided nothing and my secret
    Will remain with me, while yours is lost.
    Poor Templar! Who'd have thought you men could keep
    A secret such for long concealed from women!
TEMPLAR: What if we don't know we've one to hide?
DAYA: That may be. In which case, I must first
    Be kind enough, sir, to enlighten you.
    Why did you, in the twinkling of an eye,
    Take to your heels without a word of warning
    And leave us high and dry? Why didn't you
    Come home again with Nathan? Was it that
    Recha made so little impact on you,
    Or quite the opposite? Too much, too great!
    Was it the frantic fluttering of a bird,
    Glued to a twig? In short, confess to me
    At once, that you love Recha, love her madly!
    And I will tell you…
TEMPLAR: Madly, yes, indeed –
    You fully understand the situation.
DAYA: Only confess to me your love for her;
    The madness I don't need to know about.
TEMPLAR: Because it's obvious, you mean? It's mad
    For a Christian Knight to love a Jewish girl?
DAYA: It wouldn't seem to make much sense, that's true

But sometimes, things make better sense than we
Suppose. It's not unheard of for Our Saviour
To draw us to Him using covert paths a wise man,
On his own, would scarcely tread.

TEMPLAR: You speak
Portentously. (*Aside*.) Say Providence
Instead of Saviour and she could be right!
(*Aloud*.) You make me far more curious than normal.

DAYA: This is the land of miracles, you know!

TEMPLAR: (*Aside*.) A wondrous land. Could it be otherwise?
Where people from all over flock together?
(*Aloud*.) Dear Daya, take for granted what you wish:
That I love Recha and cannot conceive
How it were possible to live without her.

DAYA: You're certain, Knight? Then swear to me to make
Her yours for ever and to save the girl,
Here, for a time – and there, eternally.

TEMPLAR: What do you mean? How can I swear what's not
Within my power to execute?

DAYA: It is!
One word from me is all that's now required.

TEMPLAR: That Recha's father shouldn't be opposed?

DAYA: As for her father, he must be in favour.

TEMPLAR: Must? Why must he, Daya, since as yet,
The good man hasn't fallen among thieves?
He cannot be compelled.

DAYA: But he must wish it –
In the end, accept it gladly!

TEMPLAR: Must and gladly!
Let me tell you, Daya, I've already tried
To strike that chord with him.

DAYA: You cannot mean,
He wouldn't play?

TEMPLAR: He struck so harsh a discord
He insulted me.

DAYA: How so? Had you but voiced
The faintest shadow of a wish for Recha,
Would Nathan not have jumped for joy? Would he
Have frostily withdrawn into himself or

Made excuses?

TEMPLAR: More or less.

DAYA: Then I'll

Not hesitate a moment longer, but confide.

TEMPLAR: You're having second thoughts?

DAYA: In other ways,

He is so good; I owe so much to him!

I'm astonished that he wouldn't even listen!

God knows, my heart will bleed to force his hand.

TEMPLAR: Daya, I entreat you to explain!

Put an end to my uncertainty.

But if you're still in doubt about

Whether what you intend is good or evil,

Praiseworthy or disgraceful, hold your tongue –

And I'll forget you've done so.

DAYA: You incite me

Rather than restrain. It's time you knew:

Recha is not a Jewess – she's a Christian!

TEMPLAR: (*Coldly.*) Good luck to you! The birth was difficult?

Don't let a hard delivery deter you,

But zealously go on and people heaven

If you can do no more on earth!

DAYA: Sir Knight!

Does what I've said deserve no more than jibes?

Surely the fact that Recha is a Christian

Ought to rejoice your Christian heart, Sir Templar –

If you love her!

TEMPLAR: All the more because

Her Christianity is all your doing!

DAYA: That's what you think, is it? I'd like to see

A person capable of converting Recha!

It's her good fortune to have been so long

What now she can't become.

TEMPLAR: Explain – or go!

DAYA: She is a Christian, born of Christian parents

And baptised...

TEMPLAR: (*Quickly.*) And Nathan?

DAYA: He is not her father.

TEMPLAR: Not her father? Do you realise

What you're saying?

DAYA: It's the truth, which often
I've bewailed with tears of blood. But no,
He's not her father...

TEMPLAR: He just raised her as
His daughter? He reared a Christian child
As a Jewess?

DAYA: He did.

TEMPLAR: She didn't know
What she had been from birth? He never told her
She was Christian-born, not Jewish?

DAYA: Never!

TEMPLAR: It wasn't just the child he reared in this
Delusion? Equally, he left the girl
Deluded?

DAYA: Yes, alas!

TEMPLAR: But how could Nathan,
Good, wise Nathan bear to falsify
The voice of nature – grossly to mislead
A heart's effusion, which if left alone,
Would certainly have flowed another way.
Be that as it may, you have to me confided
Something of great importance which may well
Have consequences, but which has confused me
So, I can't decide at once what I should do.
Give me time to think! But leave me now!
He's coming past again and could surprise us.
Quick, be off with you!

DAYA: He'd have my life!

TEMPLAR: Just now I cannot bring myself to talk
To him. If you should meet him, tell him
Please from me, that I'll await him at
The Sultan's Palace.

DAYA: But don't let him see
You've turned against him! That would merely
Be the final straw. For Recha's sake,
You must move cautiously! And if, at last,
You take her back to Europe, you will not
Leave me behind?

TEMPLAR: That we shall see. Now, go!

End of Act Three.

ACT FOUR

Scene 1

In the cloisters of the monastery.

The BROTHER, soon joined by TEMPLAR.

BROTHER: The Patriarch is absolutely right!
 I must admit I've not had much success
 Achieving what he bade me undertake.
 Why must he always land me with such tasks?
 I'm not that subtle, nor am I persuasive;
 Don't stick my nose in other people's business;
 Hate dabbling in all the world's affairs.
 Why else would I have chosen to withdraw
 And be alone? Yet now I find myself,
 For the first time, involved – and thoroughly –
 With all and sundry, on behalf of others.
TEMPLAR: (*Approaching quickly.*)
 Good Brother! There you are, I see! Well met –
 I've been looking for you quite some time.
BROTHER: For me, Sir?
TEMPLAR: Don't say you've forgotten me?
BROTHER: Why no, indeed! Twas only that I thought
 I'd likely not catch sight of you again.
 I even prayed to God I never would!
 The good Lord knows how hard it was for me
 To carry out that task I was assigned.
 He knows I never wished you to agree,
 How I rejoiced, within my heart of hearts,
 When you unhesitatingly rejected
 What struck you as unseemly for a Knight.
 But now you're here. You've not had second thoughts?
TEMPLAR: You don't already know what brings me back?
 I hardly know myself!
BROTHER: You've reconsidered –
 Maybe you've concluded that, all said

And done, the Patriarch was not far wrong:
His proposition could bring wealth and honour.
A foe's a foe, albeit he may prove
Himself our guardian angel sevenfold.
You've pondered in cold blood and you've
Returned determined to accept? O God!

TEMPLAR: Dear pious Brother, set your mind at rest!
It's not on that account I've come today
And wish to see the Patriarch. My thoughts
Upon that issue haven't changed; nor would
I wish, for all the world, to sacrifice
The fair opinion of a man so upright,
Gentle, pious as yourself. I've merely come
To seek the Patriarch's advice upon
A matter...

BROTHER: You? Consult the Patriarch?
A Knight, a – Priest? (*Looking round nervously.*)

TEMPLAR: Why, yes – it is a priestly
matter.

BROTHER: Would any priest consult a knight,
However chivalrous the cause?

TEMPLAR: His privilege
It is to err, a privilege we don't
Much envy him. If I had none to think of,
Accountable to none but to myself,
I wouldn't need your Patriarch. However,
Certain things I'd sooner see done badly
At the behest of others, than done well
According to my will alone. The more so
Since I see religion is withal
A party matter. He who believes himself
Impartial, will adopt another's stance
Unwittingly. But since that's how it is,
So be it.

BROTHER: I would sooner hold my tongue,
For I don't rightly understand.

TEMPLAR: You do!
(*Aside.*) What is it I am really seeking here!
Orders? Advice? In general or precise?

(*Aloud.*) Brother, thank you for your useful guidance.
What need of Patriarch, when I've got you!
The Christian in the Patriarch I meant
To ask, and not the other way about.
My question is –
BROTHER: Sir, not another word!
A waste of time! You overrate me, sir.
He who knows too much has many chores –
I've vowed to concentrate on one alone!
That's lucky! Here he comes, the man himself!
You just wait here, sir. He's already seen you.

Scene 2

The PATRIARCH approaching along a cloister with ritual pomp,
TEMPLAR and BROTHER.

TEMPLAR: I'd just as soon avoid him. Not my type –
One of those friendly, fat and rosy prelates:
What splendour!!
BROTHER: You should see him dressed for Court!
Today, he's just been visiting the sick.
TEMPLAR: His garb would not shame Saladin!
PATRIARCH: (*As he draws near, makes a sign to the BROTHER.*)
Come here!
Isn't that the Templar? What's he want?
BROTHER: Don't know.
PATRIARCH: (*Goes up to TEMPLAR, while the BROTHER and
the retinue retire.*) Sir Knight, I'm very glad to meet
A brave young man! So very young, indeed!
You'll come to something, with God's help!
TEMPLAR:
I doubt,
Your Grace, if it will be much more than what
I am already; rather less, I think.
PATRIARCH: I wish, at least, that such a pious Knight
In God's good cause and of all pious folk
May long help Christianity to thrive and bloom.
That shall not fail to be, provided that

Courageous youth will heed the wise advice
Of age. And now, Sir Knight, pray tell me how
I may assist you...
TEMPLAR: By providing that,
Which, owing to my youth, I lack: advice.
PATRIARCH: Gladly, assuming the advice is followed.
TEMPLAR: Not blindly, though!
PATRIARCH: Who's saying that? It's true
None should neglect to use the reason God
Gave Man, when needed. But, you may ask, is it
Not needed at all times and everywhere?
No! For example, if the Lord saw fit –
Through one of his angels, servants of His Word –
To let us know a means whereby we might
Promote in some particular way the welfare
Of all Christians and the Church consolidate,
Who would dare subject to reason's probe
The will of Him who reason made Himself?
The everlasting laws of Heaven's glory,
Who'd try to measure by the petty rules
Of vanity? Enough of that. What makes
You seek our counsel now?
TEMPLAR: Good reverend
Father, let us just suppose a Jew
Had only one child – let it be a girl –
Whom with the greatest care he educated
In all virtuous ways – and whom he loved
More than he loved his soul, and, in return,
Was loved with love most irreproachable.
If one of us were then to be informed,
The girl was not the daughter of the Jew:
He'd found her somewhere as an infant, bought
Or stolen her, no matter which, but she
Was known to be, in fact, a Christian child –
Baptised – and that the Jew had brought her up
As a Jewess and his daughter, leaving her
Convinced that she was both – ? What would you say,
Your Eminence, had best be done in such

A situation?

PATRIARCH: I'm appalled! But tell me first:
Is this case real or hypothetical?
That is to say, did you invent it or
Did it truly happen and is this
The present situation?

TEMPLAR: I would say,
It really doesn't matter since I ask
Only your opinion?

PATRIARCH: Doesn't matter?!
There, you see how man's proud reason goes
Astray in spiritual affairs. Of course
It matters! If the case is nothing more
Than witty talking point, it isn't worth
A moment's serious thought. I would have said,
Best try the stage, where all the pros and cons,
Well argued out, could merit much applause.
However, if you're not just trying to tease me
With farcical invention – if it's fact,
If it occurred in our own diocese,
In our dear city of Jerusalem,
In that case, well then –

TEMPLAR: Well then, what?

PATRIARCH: The Jew must pay the penalty at once
And undergo the punishment decreed
By Papal and Imperial law for crime
So grave – an act of blasphemy!

TEMPLAR: Indeed?

PATRIARCH: To be precise, the laws already mentioned
Prescribe for Jews who dare seduce a Christian
To commit apostasy: being burned alive,
The stake, the pyre!

TEMPLAR: Indeed?

PATRIARCH: Especially,
When the Jew has torn a Christian child
From the embrace of its baptismal bonds!
For every act against a child is forcible -
Except, of course, acts undertaken by

The Church.

TEMPLAR: What if, without the Jew's compassion,
The baby might have perished miserably?

PATRIARCH: Even so, the Jew must burn! Better
It is to die in misery on earth
Than to be saved and so perforce condemned
To suffer for eternity. Moreover,
Why should a Jew seek to preempt God's mercy?
God can rescue whom He will, without him.

TEMPLAR: Or – I would have thought – despite him.

PATRIARCH: Even so, the Jew must burn!

TEMPLAR: It
grieves me,
All the more because, it's said, that far
From raising her in his own faith, the Jew
Instilled no faith in her at all, except
To teach her about God, no more no less.
Than would suffice for reason.

PATRIARCH: All the same,
The Jew must burn! Indeed, for that alone,
He'd merit burning three times over!
To let a child grow up without a faith?
Not teach it man's great duty to believe?
That is too wicked! I'm amazed, Sir Knight,
That you yourself...

TEMPLAR: Your Eminence,
The rest, if God so wills it, in Confession.
(*Makes a move to walk away.*)

PATRIARCH: What! You still refuse to give me details?
Won't even name the Jew, that rogue! Still less
Produce him for me here and now? I know!
I'll go and see the Sultan right away.
Saladin, by virtue of our charter,
Swore and is in duty-bound thereby
To offer us protection, to assure us
All rights and doctrines which we count forever
Part of our most holy Christian faith!
Praise God, we have his signature, his seal

On the original document. That's ours!
I'll have no trouble in persuading him
How great the danger for the state itself,
Is non-belief: all bonds of citizenship
Dissolved and torn to shreds, if man cannot
Believe in anything. A crime so heinous
Cannot be tolerated!

TEMPLAR: I regret
I haven't time just now to savour fully
A sermon so inspiring. I've been summoned
By the Sultan.

PATRIARCH: Oh... Well, then... Of course!

TEMPLAR: If you like, I'll warn him in advance,
Your Eminence.

PATRIARCH: Oh, well... I know that you've
Found favour with the Sultan. If you would,
Assure him of my very best respects.
I'm driven only by my zeal for God.
If I go too far, it's for His sake –
No doubt, Sir Knight, you will allow for that.
I take it that what you were telling me
About the Jew – was academic, as it were –
A problem –

TEMPLAR: Yes, a problem... (*Exit TEMPLAR.*)

PATRIARCH: (*Aside.*)   One which I
Must do my level best to ferret out.
It sounds to me exactly like another
Task for Brother Bonafides. (*Aloud.*) Here, my son!
(*He talks to the BROTHER as he leaves.*)

Scene 3

A room in Sultan Saladin's Palace, where SLAVES are carrying in a number of money-bags which they arrange side by side on the floor.

SALADIN, joined shortly by SITTAH.

SALADIN: (*Coming in.*)
Gracious! Is there no end to it? How much

More is still to come?

SLAVE: As much again.

SALADIN: Well, take the rest of it to Sittah. Tell me,
    Where's Al Hafi? He must now take charge
    Of all this – or, should I perhaps not send it
    To my father right away? Unless I do,
    The cash will simply dribble through my fingers.
    It's true, one finally becomes more careful;
    They'll have a job to squeeze it out of me.
    At least until the gold arrives from Egypt,
    The poor will have to do their best to manage.
    The Sepulchre's a steady source of alms;
    And Christian pilgrims when they start for home
    Won't be allowed to leave us empty-handed.
    If only –

SITTAH: What's the meaning of all this
    What's all that money doing in my room?

SALADIN: Take what's owed to you and put what's left –
    If anything remains – in store.

SITTAH: Has Nathan
    Not come back yet with the Templar?

SALADIN: He's
    Been searching for that Templar everywhere.

SITTAH: Look what I found as I was sorting through
    My jewellery and trinkets!
    (*Showing him a small portrait.*)

SALADIN: That's my brother!
    There he is – or was. It's as he was.
    The dear brave lad I had to lose so soon.
    What might I have achieved with you beside me!
    Give me the picture, Sittah. Well I know it.
    He gave it to your elder sister, Lilla,
    Who didn't want to let him leave that morning –
    The last time that he ever rode away.
    'Twas I – I sent him out and all alone.
    Lilla died of grief. She never could
    Forgive my having sent him on his own.
    He stayed away!

SITTAH: Poor brother!

SALADIN: Never mind!
   Sooner or later, all of us stay away!
   Especially – who knows? Not only Death
   Frustrates a young man's aim in life. He had
   His enemies and the strongest man
   Will often fall as swiftly as the weakest.
   Whatever happened, I must now compare
   This portrait of him with the Templar Knight;
   I want to see how far imagination
   May have cheated me.
SITTAH: That's why I brought it.
   Let me have it, though, and I will tell you;
   Woman's eye is best equipped to judge.
SALADIN: (*To a WATCHMAN who enters.*)
   Who's there? If that's the Templar, let him in!
SITTAH: Not to disturb you or to mislead him
   By seeming to be over-curious –
   (*Sits apart on the sofa and lowers her veil.*)
SALADIN: Good, that's right! (*Aside.*) Now let me hear the voice!
   For Assad's voice still slumbers in my mind…

Scene 4

TEMPLAR and SALADIN.

TEMPLAR: I, your prisoner, Sultan –
SALADIN: Prisoner?
   To him whose life I grant, would I not also
   Grant his liberty?
TEMPLAR: What you see fit to do
   Would ill become me to assume before
   I hear it. But, Sultan, it would not befit
   My status or my character to thank you
   Too profusely for my life. In any
   Case, it's at your service.
SALADIN: All I ask
   Is that you do not use your life against me.
   Gladly I'll spare my foes two extra hands;
   But I'd be loath to part with such a heart

As yours. In no way have you disappointed
Me, young man! In soul as well as body,
You are Assad. I could almost ask you
Where you've been hiding all these many years,
Immured in some sequestered cave asleep?
Or in what fairyland by some good sprite
Has this fresh flower been magically preserved?
I'm tempted to remind you of the times
When we together carried out some coup –
Could quarrel with you now for having hid
From me *one* secret, so depriving me
Of any share in *that* – your last – adventure.
That I could – if I saw only you
And not myself. At least, this much is fact
In my sweet reverie: my Autumn years
Will see a second Assad blossoming
In his Spring. Are you content with that,
Sir Knight?

TEMPLAR: Whatever you suggest to me –
Be what it may – is in my heart already
As a wish.

SALADIN: Let's put that to the test!
I take it that you'll stay with me, close by?
Whether as Christian or Moslem matters not –
In Templar's tunic or in galabiya,
Turban or helmet, as it pleases you.
It's all the same to me. I've never wished
For every tree to grow the selfsame bark.

TEMPLAR: Or else you'd hardly be what now you are:
A hero who, at heart, would sooner be
God's gardener.

SALADIN: Well, if you think no worse
Of me, we're half-agreed!

TEMPLAR: Agreed!

SALADIN: (*Offering his hand.*) Your word?

TEMPLAR: (*Shaking hands.*) Your
man! Receive from me herewith much more
Than you could ever take from me. Your servant!

SALADIN: Too great a profit in a single day!
    He's not with you?
TEMPLAR: Who?
SALADIN: Nathan.
TEMPLAR: (*Coldly.*)   I'm alone.
SALADIN: Courageous act of yours! How fortunate
    That such a deed should benefit a person
    So deserving.
TEMPLAR: Yes.
SALADIN: So cold? No, no, young man!
    When God makes use of us for good, one must
    Not be so cold, nor even wish to seem so
    Out of modesty.
TEMPLAR: Strange, in this world
    How everything has many sides to it –
    Often so many that one can't see how
    They fit together!
SALADIN: Always choose the best
    And praise the Lord; He knows how things connect!
    But if you're going to be difficult,
    Young man, it seems I, too, will need to be
    Somewhat reserved towards you. For, alas,
    I, too, have many sides which may not seem
    To harmonise too well with one another.
TEMPLAR: I'm sad to hear it. By and large, mistrust
    Is not a fault of mine.
SALADIN: Then tell me who
    It is that you mistrust. It can't be Nathan!
    You suspect *him*? Of what? Come on, explain!
    I'd like to see you prove your trust in me!
TEMPLAR: I've nothing against Nathan. It's myself
    With whom I'm furious.
SALADIN: But what about?
TEMPLAR: For dreaming that a Jew could ever learn
    How not to be one. Worst of all, I dreamt it,
    Wide awake!
SALADIN: Let's hear this day-dream, then!
TEMPLAR: You've heard of Nathan's daughter, Sultan. What
    I did for her, I did – because I did it.

Too proud to harvest thanks with nothing sown,
For days, I scorned to see the girl again.
Her father was away but back he comes,
Gets wind and seeks me out. He thanks me warmly,
Saying that he hopes I'll like his daughter,
Hints at prospects, happiness ahead,
Then talks me into visiting his home
Where waits the girl who's – Sultan, I'm ashamed!
SALADIN: Ashamed? But why? Because a Jewish girl
Impressed you, Templar? And what's wrong with that?
TEMPLAR: That my impulsive heart – inveigled by
Her father's kindly chat – opposed such slight
Resistance to that very first impression!
Simpleton, I leapt a second time
Into the fire and now it was my turn
To woo her – and my turn to be rejected.
SALADIN: How rejected?
TEMPLAR: Her wise father, true,
Did not at once dismiss me out of hand,
But wisely said he'd make inquiries first
And think about it. But was that how I
Reacted? Did I first ask questions, then
Reflect with care, when all the while the girl
Stood shrieking in the flames? All very well
By God, to be so wise, so cautious!
SALADIN: Oh, come, come!
Make some allowance for an aging father.
How long can his objections be sustained?
Do you suppose he means to stipulate
That you should first become a Jew?
TEMPLAR: Who knows?
SALADIN: Who knows? Why, one who knows this Nathan

better!
TEMPLAR: The superstitions we imbibe in youth
Don't cease to influence us even though
We see them finally for what they are.
Not all are truly free who mock their chains.
SALADIN: Well said! But surely Nathan… No, not he.
TEMPLAR: The superstition which is worst of all

Is thinking your own more bearable than others...
SALADIN: Perhaps. But Nathan...
TEMPLAR: ...And the only guide
    Dim-sighted humankind can count upon –
    Till eyes grow fit to face the blaze of truth –
    The only guide...
SALADIN: Quite so! But this is not
    Our Nathan's weakness –
TEMPLAR: So I thought! But if
    Instead, this paragon turns out to be
    A common or garden Jew who even hunts
    For Christian infants with the end in view
    Of educating them as Jews – what then?
SALADIN: Who's accusing him of that?
TEMPLAR: The girl
    With whom he lured me, keen it seemed
    To offer me her hand as my reward –
    That what I'd done for her be not in vain –
    This very girl is not our Nathan's daughter,
    But some stray Christian child he found –
SALADIN:
    Whom he,
    Despite that, will not let you marry?
TEMPLAR: Whether he will or won't, he's been unmasked!
    His tolerant blether shown for what it's worth!
    I'll set the hounds about this Jewish wolf
    In philosophical sheep-skin. They will fleece him!
SALADIN: (*Solemnly.*)
    Gently, Christian!
TEMPLAR: Gently? What do you mean?
    If Jew and Moslem both insist on being
    Themselves, should only Christian be denied
    That right?
SALADIN: (*Even more solemn.*) Gently, Christian!

TEMPLAR: (*Calmly.*)　　　　　　I can feel
　　The weighty burden of reproach compressed
　　By Saladin in those two words. If only
　　I could know how Assad would react,
　　Were he in my position!
SALADIN:　　　　　Not much better!
　　Equally hot-headed, I suspect!
　　Who taught you, though, to prick me with *one* word –
　　As Assad, too, knew how? I must admit,
　　If things are as you say, then Nathan wouldn't
　　Be the man I thought him – yet, he's still
　　My friend. I cannot bear my friends to be
　　At loggerheads among themselves! Go easy!
　　Take my advice: don't hurry to expose him
　　To the zealots of your rabble; not to speak
　　Of the pressure which your clergy would exert
　　On me, to be revenged on him! Just be
　　A Christian, spiting neither Jew nor Moslem!
TEMPLAR: Your words have very nearly come too late!
　　The blood-lust of the Patriarch, however,
　　Warned me in time not to become his tool.
SALADIN: You mean you went to see the Patriarch
　　Before you came to me?
TEMPLAR:　　　　In passion's storm,
　　Bemused by indecision! Please forgive me!
　　Henceforth, I fear, you'll not discern in me
　　Much likeness to your brother.
SALADIN:　　　　　　That's precisely
　　What I feared! But well I know the faults
　　From which true virtue sprouts. Just cultivate
　　The virtue and the faults won't greatly
　　Mar my view of you. Now, go find Nathan,
　　As he searched for you, and bring him here,
　　For I must swiftly reconcile you both.
　　If you are serious about the girl, rest easy!
　　She is yours! And Nathan will perceive
　　That, even without pork, it's possible
　　To raise a Christian child! Now go!

(*Exit the TEMPLAR. SITTAH leaves the sofa.*)

Scene 5

SALADIN and SITTAH.

SITTAH: It's quite
    Astonishing!
SALADIN: Isn't it? Do you not agree –
    My Assad must have been a fine young man!
SITTAH: He must indeed have been! Or one might think
    The Templar was the subject of this portrait!
    But how was it that you forgot to ask
    About his parents?
SALADIN: In particular,
    His mother, don't you think? And whether she
    Was never in these parts?
SITTAH: Do please find out.
SALADIN: It's more than possible, I'd say. Our Assad
    Was always well received by pretty Christian
    Ladies and he himself so much a ladies' man
    With pretty Christians, rumour had it once –
    But come – less said about all that the better!
    Enough I have him back with all his faults,
    The moods and tantrums of a tender heart!
    Oh, Nathan really must give him the girl!
    Don't you agree?
SITTAH: Why *give* her to him?
    Rather leave her with him!
SALADIN: True enough!
    What right has he, if he is not her father?
    He who saved her life's the one entitled
    To exercise the right of him who sired her.
SITTAH: Why then, Saladin, should you not take
    The maiden quickly under your protection,
    Removing her for good from her illegal
    Owner?
SALADIN: Is there any need for that?
SITTAH: Need? Perhaps not. It was curiosity –

But kindly meant – that prompted my advice.
The truth is, in the case of certain men,
I like to know as soon as possible
The sort of girl they fall for.

SALADIN: That being so,
Why don't you send for her?

SITTAH: Oh, really? May I?

SALADIN: Careful with Nathan, though! On no account
Must he suspect that we intend to take
The girl by force.

SITTAH: Don't worry!

SALADIN: I, meanwhile,
Must go and see what's happened to Al Hafi.

Scene 6

As in Act One, Scene 1: the open porch of Nathan's villa, looking
towards the palm-grove. Part of his merchandise and valuables
lie unpacked and are under discussion.

NATHAN and DAYA.

DAYA: It's all so wonderful! The choicest stuff!
Presents which only you know how to give!
Where do they make this lovely silver ware,
With golden filagree? Must cost the earth!
My word! Here's what I call a wedding-gown!
Magnificent! What queen could ask for more?

NATHAN: Wedding gown, you say? Why wedding-gown?

DAYA: What else? Perhaps it wasn't what you planned
When buying it. But Nathan, mark my words,
That's what it's got to be and nothing less –
A wedding garment made to order: white –
For innocence – and all these bands of gold,
Wound in and out to symbolise great wealth!
Just look at it! The loveliest of gowns!

NATHAN: What do you mean by teasing me? Whose wedding
Dress are you so expertly presenting?
Are you the bride?

DAYA: Me?

NATHAN: Then, who else?

DAYA: Dear God!

NATHAN: Who then? Who else's wedding gown is this?
    It's meant for you! It's yours – and no-one else's!

DAYA: For me? It's mine? This dress is not for Recha?

NATHAN: Why, no! The present I have brought for her
    Is in another bale. Pack up and go –
    Take all your bits and pieces with you!

DAYA: Tempter!
    Even were these the costliest goods on earth,
    I'd still not touch them till you swear to me
    Not to let pass this opportunity.
    Heaven will never send another like it!

NATHAN: Not let pass? An opportunity? For what?

DAYA: Don't pretend you do not understand!
    The Templar Knight loves Recha. Let him have her!
    And then your sin, which I dare hide no longer,
    Will be at last absolved. The girl, once more
    Mid fellow-Christians, can become what she
    Still is, and yet remain what she's become.
    And you, with all your generosity
    To us, for which we cannot thank you fully,
    Will not have merely heaped upon your head
    Coals of fire!

NATHAN: The same old tune! Although,
    The lyre has one new string which, I'm afraid,
    Is neither true nor taut.

DAYA: What do you mean?

NATHAN: I'm much in favour of the Templar and would sooner
    He than anyone on earth were wed to Recha –
    Except that... No, just wait. Have patience!

DAYA: Patience?
    Nathan, isn't that the same old tune
    You've played for years?

NATHAN: A few more days be patient!
    Look, who's coming! Isn't that a monk?
    Go ask him what he wants!

DAYA: What *would* he want?

(*She goes up to him and asks.*)
NATHAN: Give – don't wait for him to ask you first!
(*Aside.*) If only I could sound the Templar out
Without explaining why it is I'm curious!
Were I to tell him, only then to find
That my suspicions were unjust, I would
Have parted with my secret needlessly...
(*Aloud.*) What does he want?
DAYA: He'd like to speak to you.
NATHAN: Then show him in, by all means. You may leave us.

Scene 7

NATHAN and the BROTHER.

NATHAN: (*Aside.*) I'd so much like to stay as Recha's father –
But couldn't I still be that, in fact, although
No longer known as such to all and sundry?
Recha will surely always call me father,
Once she's aware how much I wish I were!
(*Aloud.*) Welcome! What can I do to help you, Brother?
BROTHER: Not very much. But I am glad to see you
Once again, Lord Nathan.
NATHAN: Do you know me?
BROTHER: Indeed! Who doesn't know you hereabouts?
Your name's been printed on so many palms –
My own included – for so many years.
NATHAN: (*Reaching for his purse.*)
Let me refresh the image, Brother!
BROTHER: Thanks,
But, no! I'll not rob those who're poorer still!
If you will just allow me to refresh
Your memory of *my* name, for I can claim
Once to have placed in *your* hands long ago
Something of value, not to be despised.
NATHAN: Forgive me! I'm ashamed. I can't recall...
Remind me, please and, for my penance, let
Me now repay you sevenfold.
BROTHER: But first

155

And foremost, I must tell you, I myself
Only today was suddenly reminded
Of the pledge I left with you.

NATHAN: What pledge was that?

BROTHER: Not long ago, when I was still a hermit,
At Quarantana, close to Jericho,
A band of Arab robbers smashed my shrine,
Wrecked my cell and carried me away.
Luckily, I managed to escape
And here, took refuge with the Patriarch,
Seeking another spot where, all alone,
I might serve God in peace until my days
Were done.

NATHAN: Good Brother, I'm on tenterhooks;
The pledge! This pledge you say you left with me?

BROTHER: Presently, Lord Nathan! You shall hear!
The Patriarch promised me a hermitage
On Tabor soon as it fell vacant but
Meanwhile, I was to stay here as a Brother.
And here I am and pining every day,
A hundred times, for Tabor's solitude.
The Patriarch makes use of me for tasks
Of every kind which I dislike intensely.
For example:

NATHAN: Please get to the point!

BROTHER: Almost there! It seems he's been informed
That a Jew who lives not very far away
Has raised a Christian baby as his daughter.

NATHAN: (*Flabbergasted.*)
What?!

BROTHER: Just hear me out! He's ordered me
Without delay, to trace this Jew for him.
He's beside himself with fury at a crime
He calls the sin against the Holy Ghost –
That is to say, as we believe, the greatest
Sin of all but, thank the Lord, we still
Don't know quite what that grievous sin entails.
Well, suddenly, my conscience was aroused

And it occurred to me that I myself
Could possibly have occasioned years ago
This unforgivably grave offence to God!
Tell me, did not – some eighteen years long past –
A rider bring a baby girl to you?
NATHAN: What do you mean? Well, yes – in fact –
BROTHER:
Look hard
At me. I am myself that self-same groom!
NATHAN: You
are?
BROTHER: The gentleman whose child it was –
If I can trust my memory – was named
Wolf von Filnek!
NATHAN: That's correct!
BROTHER: The mother
Had died not long before and, since
The father had been posted suddenly
To Gaza, where he couldn't take a child,
He sent her to yourself. Did I not meet you
With the baby in Darun?
NATHAN: Indeed you did!
BROTHER: Twould be no wonder, if my memory
Deceived. I had so many worthy masters,
And I was Filnek's servant only briefly.
Soon after, he was killed at Askalon,
But was, it seems, well-loved.
NATHAN: Indeed he was!
I owed so much to him for, more than once,
His intervention saved me from the sword.
BROTHER: I'm glad to hear it! Then his daughter must
Have been that much more welcome in your home…
NATHAN: As you can well imagine.
BROTHER: Then, where is she?
It cannot be that she has died meanwhile?
Oh, let her not be dead! If no-one else
Knows anything of this, then all may yet
Be well.
NATHAN: You think so?

BROTHER: Trust me, Nathan!
   This is how I see it: if the good
   I seek to do, too closely borders on
   A crime, then I would sooner not do good.
   On evil, we're reliably informed,
   But far from knowing all about what's good.
   Twould be quite natural for a Christian child
   To be well raised by you; as though she were
   Your own young daughter, reared with love
   And fatherly devotion. Should you be
   Rewarded in this fashion? I say no!
   You might have acted more astutely had you
   Let her be raised a Christian by
   Another. But if you had, then you would not
   Have loved your good friend's baby daughter.
   Children have greater need of love – were it
   But that of animals – than they have need
   Of Christianity when they are little.
   For Christianity, there's time enough...
   Provided, in your care, the girl has grown
   Healthy and God-fearing, she'll remain
   In God's eyes what she always was – a Christian.
   Is Christianity, all said and done,
   Not built on Judaism? Often I've
   Been moved to anger, copious tears have shed,
   That Christians are so ready to forget
   Our own Lord Jesus was himself a Jew!
NATHAN: Good Brother, you will have to speak for me
   Should hatred and hypocrisy combine
   Against me for my deed – and what a deed!
   You and you alone shall know of it.
   But you must take my secret to the grave.
   By vanity I've so far not been tempted
   To breathe it to a soul. Only to you
   I'll tell it. Pious simplicity alone
   Shall hear the tale, for only piety
   Can comprehend what deeds can be performed
   By man submissive to the will of God.
BROTHER: You're deeply moved. I see tears welling up.
NATHAN: You met me with the baby in Darun.

I don't believe you knew, but days before,
In Gath, the Christians massacred the Jews –
Women and children, too. Nor could you know,
Among them were my wife and seven sons
Who'd taken refuge in my brother's house,
Where they were burned alive.

BROTHER: Oh, God almighty!

NATHAN: When you arrived, I'd lain three days and nights
Alone, in dust and ashes, weeping before God –
Arguing with God... I raged and ranted.
The world and myself I cursed and vowed lifelong
To hate all Christendom.

BROTHER: No wonder!

NATHAN: But reason gradually gained the upper hand.
Its gentle voice proclaimed 'Yet God exists!
That, too, was his decree. So brace yourself!
Come, practise what you've long well understood –
That which is no more difficult to practise
Than to comprehend – if you'll but try.
Stand up!' I stood and cried to God, 'I will,
If it be Your will I should!' And then
You came, dismounted and consigned to me
A baby swaddled in your cloak. What you
Then said to me and I to you, I have forgot.
I only know I put the child to bed
And kissed it. Then I knelt and sobbed, 'Oh, God,
For seven lost, here's one returned.'

BROTHER: O Nathan!
You're a Christian! As God lives, a Christian!
There never was a better one!

NATHAN: You see:
What makes me Christian in your eyes is that
Which makes you seem a Jew in mine! But hold,
Let's not enfeeble one another now.
It's time for us to act! As seven-fold love
Soon bound me to that single unknown child,
I cannot bear the thought that, losing her,
I'll once more lose my seven sons – but if
The will of Providence demands that I
Surrender her, why then – I shall obey!

BROTHER: Brave soul! That was the counsel I myself
 Had thought to offer you. Your noble heart
 Advised you in advance!
NATHAN: However, let
 The first chance-comer not presume that he
 Can rob me of the girl!
BROTHER: Why, no indeed!
NATHAN: He who has no greater rights upon her
 Than I, must have some former ties –
BROTHER: Agreed!
NATHAN: Conferred on him by nature and by blood.
BROTHER: I think so, too.
NATHAN: So, quickly name a brother,
 Uncle, cousin or some relative!
 I shall not withold her from him – she
 Who was born and educated to enhance
 Whatever family of whatever faith.
 I trust you may know more than I about
 Your former master and his kith and kin.
BROTHER: I fear I cannot help you much, good Nathan,
 For, as you've heard, my time with him was brief.
NATHAN: But do you not at least have some idea
 About his mother? Was she not a Stauffen?
BROTHER: That could well be. I think she was…
NATHAN: Her brother…
 Conrad von Stauffen? Wasn't he a Templar?
BROTHER: If I'm not mistaken… Wait a moment!
 I think I have a little book of his.
 I took it from his shirt at Askalon
 When we were burying his body.
NATHAN: And?
BROTHER: A book of prayers. A breviary, we call it.
 I thought some Christian might make use of it.
 No use to me. I cannot read it.
NATHAN: Well?
BROTHER: Well, in this book are written, front and back,
 As I've been told, and in the master's hand,
 A list of all the names of family members –
 His and hers.

NATHAN: The very thing! Go, fetch it!
Quick! To me, that's worth its weight in gold
And you shall have a thousand thanks besides!
Away you go! Be quick! Run!
BROTHER: That I will!
But what the master wrote inside that book
Is Arabic. (*Exit BROTHER.*)
NATHAN: No matter. Just you fetch it!
God, if I could only keep the girl
And with the book, procure myself, as well,
So fine a son-in-law! Too much to hope!
Be that as maybe, but I wonder who
It was that told the Patriarch the story.
I mustn't fail to ask around. What if
Our Daya was the source?

Scene 8

DAYA and NATHAN.

DAYA: (*Hurriedly, embarrassed.*) Just think!
NATHAN: What
now?
DAYA: It gave the poor girl a tremendous fright!
A messenger...
NATHAN: The Patriarch?
DAYA: No. Sittah!
The Sultan's sister –
NATHAN: Not the Patriarch?
DAYA: No! Sittah! Can't you hear? The Princess Sittah!
She sent someone here to fetch her –
NATHAN: Who?
She sent for Recha? Sittah sent for her?
Well, if the Princess Sittah sent for her
And not the Patriarch...
DAYA: Why ever should he?
NATHAN: Have you not had word from him of late?
You're sure? You haven't been confiding in him?
DAYA: Me? Him?

NATHAN: Where are the messengers?
DAYA: Outside.
NATHAN: For safety's sake, I'll speak to them myself.
    Come on! I hope the Patriarch is not
    Behind all this!
    (*Exit NATHAN.*)
DAYA: And I fear something very different!
    The only daughter – as she's thought to be –
    Of such a wealthy Jew would be by no
    Means unattractive to a Moslem.
    That would put paid to all the Templar's hopes –
    Unless I dare to take the second step
    And finally tell the girl just who she is.
    Take heart! The first time I can catch the girl
    Alone, I'll make good use of the occasion.
    It could be now, if I accompany her…
    At least a little warning in advance
    Before we get there will not come amiss.
    That's it! My mind's made up! It's now or never!
    (*Exit after NATHAN.*)

End of Act Four.

ACT FIVE

Scene 1

The room in Saladin's Palace in which the money-bags were deposited and are still to be seen.

SALADIN, later joined by several MAMELUKES.

SALADIN: (*Entering.*)
  The money is still here and no-one knows
  Where to find the Dervish; I suspect
  He came across a chess-game on his way –
  Enough for him to totally forget
  Himself and me, too. Patience! Yes, what now?
FIRST MAMELUKE: Sultan, long-awaited news! Rejoice!
  The caravan from Cairo has arrived
  Unharmed and loaded with the seven yearly
  Tribute from the bounteous River Nile.
SALADIN: Brave Ibrahim! No messenger more welcome!
  At last! At last! A thousand thanks for this
  Good news!
FIRST MAMELUKE: (*Expectantly, aside.*) Well, hand it over!
SALADIN: What are you waiting for? Be on your way!
FIRST MAMELUKE: Nothing for a messenger so welcome?
SALADIN: Why should there be?
FIRST MAMELUKE: Don't I deserve a tip?
  Am I to be the first that Saladin
  Rewarded only with a word of thanks?
  Fame at last! Am I to be the first
  With whom the Sultan has been niggardly?
SALADIN: Then help yourself to one of those money-bags.
FIRST MAMELUKE: You're sure you don't want me to

  take the lot?
SALADIN: What insolence! You've taken two! He means it!
  He's trying to outdo me in largesse!

No doubt, he finds it harder to refuse
Than I to give. What has come over me?
Why so soon before my days are ended
Should I so suddenly wish to change my style?
If I don't want to die as Saladin,
As Saladin, then, neither should I live.
SECOND MAMELUKE:
   O Sultan!
SALADIN: If you've come here to report...
SECOND MAMELUKE: The caravan has just arrived from

   Egypt!
SALADIN: That, I know.
SECOND MAMELUKE: So I'm too late!
SALADIN: Why so?
   Your good intention earns you a reward:
   Here, take a purse or two, then –
SECOND MAMELUKE: Make it three!
SALADIN: All right, if you can count! Just help yourself!
SECOND MAMELUKE: A third man's on his way, if he can

   make it –
SALADIN: How so?
SECOND MAMELUKE: Fact is, he likely broke his neck.
   The moment we three heard the gold was coming.
   We sprang to horse and off we rode to tell you.
   The first man fell, so I then took the lead
   And stayed ahead till we were in the town,
   Where Ibrahim, that loudmouth, better knows
   His way about the lanes.
SALADIN: The man who fell –
   What has become of him? Ride back and meet him!
SECOND MAMELUKE: Right willingly! And, if he's still alive,
   Half of this purse I'm taking shall be his.
   (*Exit SECOND MAMELUKE.*)
SALADIN: What a decent, open-hearted fellow!

Who's got better mamelukes than I?
And wouldn't I be justified in thinking
Twas my example helped to make them so?
Perish the thought that in my final days
They'd have to grow accustomed to a change...
THIRD MAMELUKE: Sultan...
SALADIN: Are you the one who fell?
THIRD MAMELUKE: No, sire.
I've come to let you know Emir Mansour,
The leader of the caravan's dismounted...
SALADIN: Then bring him in at once. Make haste!
Ah, there he is!

Scene 2

EMIR MANSOUR and SALADIN.

SALADIN: Emir, I bid you welcome!
What was the journey like? Mansour! Mansour!
You certainly made us wait!
MANSOUR: This letter here
Explains how first your captain Abdelkassem
Had to quell disturbances in Thebes
Before we dared set out across the desert.
I did my best, as soon as we got started,
To speed the progress of our caravanserai.
SALADIN: I'm sure you did, my good Mansour! But now,
Without delay and willingly, I trust,
I want you to relieve your weary escort
With fresh troops – take as many as you need –
And right away make haste to Lebanon
With gold which you'll deliver to my father.
MANSOUR: Very well!
SALADIN: Make sure your escort's strong
Enough. The Lebanon's no longer safe.
You may perhaps have heard, the Templar Knights
Are active yet again – so you beware!
Come show me where your caravan is waiting.
I'd like to see it and make sure that all's

In order. After that, I'll be with Sittah.

Scene 3

The palm-grove in front of Nathan's villa, with the TEMPLAR
walking to and fro.

TEMPLAR: I won't go back inside that house again;
    He's bound to reappear before too long.
    They used to notice me so swiftly and
    With pleasure. Surely he would not deny
    Himself the chance to catch me hovering
    Outside his own front door? But I am also
    Very angry with the Jew. Why is it, though,
    That I've become so bitter? He himself
    Indeed, said he'd not ruled me out.
    And Saladin has promised he'll persuade him.
    Can it be, in me, the Christian's rooted
    More deeply even than in him, the Jew?
    Who knows his own heart? But why else would I
    Begrudge him so the paltry prey he snatched
    From Christianity? Not paltry, though,
    A creature such! Magnificent! But whose?
    Not the slave's who, on life's desolate
    Shore, landed a block of wood and then escaped.
    But rather of the artist who, in that
    Abandoned block of wood, a godly figure
    Saw, which he then sculpted... Recha's true
    Father, never mind the Christian Knight
    Who sired her, will remain the Jew for ever!
    Were I to see her merely as a Christian
    Wench and disregard what I assume a Jew
    The like of Nathan could instil in her –
    Speak, my heart! What would you find to love?
    Little enough! Even her smile would be
    No more than the pretty twitching of a muscle –
    And that which made her smile, unworthy
    Of the charm bestowed upon it by her lips.
    No, indeed, it wouldn't be her smile!

I've seen smiles squandered, even lovelier still,
On vanity, empty prattle, mockery,
On flattery, frippery and flirtation, too!
Was I then captivated by her smile?
Did it inspire in me a wish to fritter
My life away with basking in its rays?
I think not. Yet I rage against the man
Who, all alone, endowed her with great virtue?
Why and how? Did I deserve the scorn
Of Saladin as he dismissed me? That he
Should think I did, was surely bad enough!
How petty then must I have seemed to him,
And how contemptible! All for a girl?
Come, Templar, this won't do! Control yourself!
What if Daya's tale was tittle-tattle,
Difficult to prove? Why, here at last,
He's coming out, and deep in conversation.
But who's this with him? It's my brother monk!
Ha, he's in the know – has probably
By now betrayed all to the Patriarch.
Fool that I am! The mischief I have caused!
To think a single spark of passion's fire
Can so burn out the fabric of one's brain!
Quick! Now decide what's best to do! I'll wait
Here out of sight and see what happens –
It may be that the Brother will now leave him.

Scene 4

NATHAN and the BROTHER.

NATHAN: (*Approaching him.*)
    Good Brother, please accept my thanks once more!
BROTHER: And you, sir, likewise.
NATHAN: I? Your thanks?
    What for?
    For being so selfish as to force on you
    Something you didn't need? You might have merely
    Bowed to my will – and readily – without

So forcefully rejecting rich reward…

BROTHER: I'm not the owner of the book. It's hers –
  The daughter's – hers alone. It was her father's
  Sole bequest. Not quite; there was yourself.
  May God but grant that you may never have
  Reason to regret you did so much for her!

NATHAN: That, I could never rue, most certainly!
  You needn't worry!

BROTHER: Ah, but hear me out –
  These Patriarchs and Templars…

NATHAN: Could never
  Damage me to such extent that I'd
  Rue any act of mine – that, least of all!
  But are you quite convinced it was the Templar
  Who put your Patriarch up to this?

BROTHER: Who else?
  A Templar came to see him just before.
  From what I've heard, seems very likely…

NATHAN: Yet –
  There's only one Templar in Jerusalem
  And him I know: he is a friend of mine,
  A youthful, honest, upright man –

BROTHER: Just so!
  The very same! But what one is and how
  One's forced to be in this world sometimes differ.

NATHAN: Yes, alas! So let him do his best
  Or worst – and be him whomsoever he may choose:
  Armed with your book, Brother, I will defy
  Them all. I'm going to the Sultan right away…

BROTHER: The best of luck! But I shall leave you here.

NATHAN: And you've not even seen her! Come again
  To visit us, soon as you can! As well
  If the Patriarch heard nothing of all this
  Today… No matter, though; say what you want.
  Even today!

BROTHER: Not I! Farewell! (*Exit.*)

NATHAN: Good Brother,
  Don't forget us! Would that I might fall
  To my knees beneath the open sky,

Feeling that anxious knot which for so long
Oppressed me, by itself unravelling.
God, how light I feel that I have now
No secret burden to conceal, that I
Can walk the world as freely among men
As in your sight, O Lord, who alone need not
Assess and judge a man by actions only –
Actions which so seldom are his own!

Scene 5

NATHAN and the TEMPLAR who approaches from the side.

TEMPLAR: Hi, Nathan! Wait! Will you not take me with you?
NATHAN: Who's calling? Templar, is it you? Where were you,
    I thought that we were meeting at the Palace.
TEMPLAR: We must have missed each other. Don't be
                                    angry!
NATHAN: Not I, but Saladin…
TEMPLAR: You'd just gone out.
NATHAN: So, then, you've talked to him. That's very good.
TEMPLAR: He wants to see the pair of us together.
NATHAN: So much the better. Come! I'm on my way
    To see him now.
TEMPLAR: Good Nathan, may I ask
    Who was it that just left you?
NATHAN: Don't you know him?
TEMPLAR: Was it not Haut, the good lay-brother, whom
    The Patriarch uses as his terrier?
NATHAN: Could be. The Patriarch employs him, I believe.
TEMPLAR: No bad idea to send simplicity
    To sniff the way ahead for villainy.
NATHAN: Stupidity to piety preferred?
TEMPLAR: No Patriarch believes in piety!
NATHAN: I'll vouch that monk won't help his Patriarch
    With any enterprise of disrepute.
TEMPLAR: At least, that's what he leads one to believe.
    But didn't he mention me at all?
NATHAN: Why you?
    Certainly not by name and I suspect

Your name would hardly be familiar.

TEMPLAR: Hardly.

NATHAN: He did say something, true, about a Templar.

TEMPLAR: What was that?

NATHAN: It couldn't have been you.

TEMPLAR: Who knows? Please tell me.

NATHAN: Someone, so he said –
A Templar – had denounced me to his Grace.

TEMPLAR: *You*? That, if I may say so, is a lie!
Listen, Nathan! I am not the man
To disavow what I have said or done.
What I have done, I've done! But, equally,
I'm not the sort to vigorously defend
My every act as irreproachable.
Why should I be ashamed of my mistakes
If it's my firm resolve to rectify them?
As if I didn't know what progress man
Can make by such amends. Please hear me, Nathan!
It's true, I am the Brother's Templar who
Was said to have accused you. Well you know
What vexed me so – what made my temper seethe.
Fool that I was! I went to you prepared,
Body and soul, to fall into your arms.
How coldly you received me! How luke-warm –
Even worse than cold – was your response!
How carefully you sought to put me off,
Seeming to answer me with random questions.
I still can't see how I could be expected
To listen calmly. Hear me, Nathan please!
While I was in a ferment, Daya crept
Upon me and surprised me with her secret
Which, I thought, explained your puzzling
Behaviour.

NATHAN: How so?

TEMPLAR: Nathan, hear me out!
I thought that, having won her from the Christians,
You were in no mood to see your Recha
Wed a Christian. It occurred to me
Therefore, to place, as it were, a knife against

Your throat, and force you – short and sweet!
NATHAN: Short and sweet! I fail to see what's sweet
About it!
TEMPLAR: Hear me, Nathan! I admit
That I was wrong and you were not to blame.
Daya, the foolish woman, didn't know
What she was saying – hates you and so tried
To implicate you in a wicked scheme.
It may be so and I – a youthful clown,
An over eager meddler on both sides –
Now doing far too much, now far too little –
That, too, may be. Forgive me, Nathan.
NATHAN: Since
That's how you see me –
TEMPLAR: In a word,
I went to the Patriarch but didn't name you.
As I have said, he lied. I just outlined
The case in very general terms and asked
The Patriarch to give me his opinion.
I'd have done better not to. I agree.
Did I not know the Patriarch's a scoundrel?
Why didn't I have it out with you directly?
Why expose the poor girl to the risk
Of losing such a father? What's the good?
The villainy of the Patriarch, unchanged,
Has brought me to my senses. Nathan, listen!
Whether he does or doesn't know your name,
He can only take the girl away
If she belongs to no-one but yourself –
Could drag her from your house to convent cloister.
So, give her to me – no-one else but me!
Then, let him come! Ha! He would never dare
To take my wife from me. But give her to me
Now! Whether she *is* your daughter or she *isn't*;
Let her be Christian, Jewish or whatever!
It matters not! I shall not question you
On this point now or ever, if I live
To be a hundred!
NATHAN: Do you think I judge it

Vital for me to conceal the truth?

TEMPLAR: Be that as may be!

NATHAN: I have never yet –
To you or anyone whose right concern it was –
Denied that Recha is a Christian and
My foster-daughter – nothing more or less.
But why then did I never tell her so?
To her alone I need apologise.

TEMPLAR: Nor is there any need where she's
concerned.
Grant her the joy of never seeing you in
Any different light. Spare her the shock
Of that discovery. You now have only
To consult her wishes. Give her to me,
Nathan, I beg of you. Give her to me!
No-one but I can rescue her a second time
And that I will.

NATHAN: Perhaps you might have done;
It's now too late.

TEMPLAR: Why? How too late?

NATHAN: Thanks
To the Patriarch…

TEMPLAR: Why thanks to him?
Thanks, what for? He's earned no thanks from us!

NATHAN: That we now know to whom she is related
And to whom she can be safely handed over.

TEMPLAR: I thank him – who could thank the man for
more?

NATHAN: From other hands than mine you must receive
Your bride.

TEMPLAR: Poor Recha! What misfortunes
Press upon you! This would be a boon
For other orphans, but for you, poor Recha,
A catastrophe! Nathan, where are they, then,
These relatives?

NATHAN: You ask me where?

TEMPLAR: And who?

NATHAN: They've found one brother in particular;
You'll have to seek her hand from him.

TEMPLAR: A brother?
  What is this brother, then? A soldier, is he?
  Or a priest? I need to know what lies
  Ahead of me.
NATHAN: I think he's neither, though
  He could be both; I don't yet know him well.
TEMPLAR: What else about him?
NATHAN: He's an honest man
  With whom dear Recha won't be badly off.
TEMPLAR: A Christian, though. I'm rather at a loss:
  I must admit, I cannot make you out.
  Don't misunderstand me, Nathan, but
  Once she's back with Christians will she not
  Herself be forced to play the Christian?
  And what she plays for long enough won't she
  Become? Will not the pure wheat you have sown
  Be choked to death at last by weeds? But you
  Don't seem to be the least concerned!
  You can even bring yourself to say
  That, with this new-found brother, Recha won't
  Be badly off?
NATHAN: I think – I hope. But if
  Perchance, she lacks for anything, she'll still
  Have you and me to call upon.
TEMPLAR: How could
  She lack for anything? Won't little brother
  Richly meet her every need – for food
  And clothes, with dainty dishes and, no doubt,
  Fine dresses – all that little sister
  May require. What more could little sister
  Ask for? Possibly a husband, but that, too,
  The brother, when it suits him, will provide;
  There's always husbands somewhere to be found!
  The more of a Christian, naturally, the better!
  O Nathan, what an angel you have formed –
  Only to have your work undone by others.
NATHAN: No need for that! The angel will not cease
  To be deserving of our love.
TEMPLAR: Oh, no!

Don't speak so of *my* love! For none shall steal
A morsel of it – no – however small!
Nor steal my name! But hold! Does she suspect
What's going on?

NATHAN: It's possible, though I
Can't think where from.

TEMPLAR: No matter, but she should –
She must – hear first from me about this twofold
Threat. I know, I swore I'd neither see
Nor speak to her again till she was mine.
That, I renounce. I'm going…

NATHAN: Where?

TEMPLAR: To her!
To find out if the girl is man enough
To take the one decision worthy of her.

NATHAN: What is that?

TEMPLAR: To ask no more about
You or her brother –

NATHAN: And?

TEMPLAR: To follow me,
Albeit at the risk of being made
To wed a Moslem.

NATHAN: Stay! She's not at home.
She's now with Sittah, sister of the Sultan.

TEMPLAR: Since when? What for?

NATHAN: And if you want to meet
The brother with them, come with me!

TEMPLAR: Whose brother? Sittah's, do you mean – or

Recha's?

NATHAN: Could easily be both. Quick! Come along!
(*Leads him out.*)

Scene 6

In Sittah's harem.

SITTAH and RECHA engaged in conversation.

SITTAH: How very glad I am, my dear, to meet you!
  But don't be shy, so timid, so reserved:
  Relax and chat; you can confide in me.
RECHA: Princess!
SITTAH: No need for titles; call me Sittah.
  Let me be your friend, your sister, call me
  Mother! Indeed, I very nearly could be
  That – so young, intelligent and pious!
  There's nothing you don't know about, you must
  Have read a vast amount!
RECHA: Read? What, me?
  Sittah, you mock your silly little sister.
  I can hardly read.
SITTAH: Oh, what a fib!
RECHA: A little, if it's in my father's hand –
  Books, I thought you meant!
SITTAH: Yes, books – of course.
RECHA: No, books are really hard for me to read.
SITTAH: You're serious?
RECHA: Completely. Father sets
  Little store by cold book-learning which,
  He says, imprints itself upon the brain
  Through lifeless symbols.
SITTAH: What a thing to say!
  Not that he's entirely wrong! So much
  Of what you know is…?
RECHA: By his word of mouth
  And most of it, I couldn't say for sure
  How, where or why he taught me.
SITTAH: It's a fact:
  That way, things register more easily,
  Enlightening one's spirit as a whole.
RECHA: I'm sure that you, yourself, read very little.
SITTAH: Why? Not that I can boast the opposite,
  What gives you that impression? Out with it!
RECHA: You are so straightforward – genuine!
  So much an individual…
SITTAH: And?

RECHA: Books,
  My father says, so rarely make one so.
SITTAH: Oh, he must be a splendid man, your father!
RECHA: I agree!
SITTAH: His observations are
  So very apt!
RECHA: I quite agree with you.
  But this same father –
SITTAH: What my dear?
RECHA: This father…
SITTAH: Lord! You're crying!
RECHA: Sorry, truth must out!
  My heart is suffocating! Give me air!
  (*Overcome by tears, throws herself at feet of SITTAH.*)
SITTAH: Has something happened, Recha?
RECHA: This
  dear father
  I'm to lose!
SITTAH: To lose him? Lose your father?
  How? Calm down! That cannot be! Stand up!
RECHA: Could that your offer to become my friend –
  My sister – weren't in vain!
SITTAH: I am! I am!
  Stand up or I shall have to summon help!
RECHA: (*Regaining control of herself, stands up.*)
  Forgive me! I'm so sorry! Please excuse me!
  Overcome by grief, I quite forgot
  That you're the Sultan's sister before whom
  Whimpering and despair are out of place.
  The cool, calm voice of reason – that alone
  Will move you and I know, whoever pleads
  His case with moderation and restraint
  Will win the day!
SITTAH: Well, then?
RECHA: My friend, my sister,
  Don't allow them! Don't let them impose
  Another father on me, please, I beg!
SITTAH: Impose another father on you? Who
  Would ever wish to do so – even try

RECHA: Who? My good, bad Daya could well wish it,
And wishes she were able! You don't know
This good, bad Daya, do you? God forgive her!
God reward her, too, for she has done
As much to help me, as to do me harm.
SITTAH: Harm you? How? If so, there can't be much
That's good about her.
RECHA: Oh, but, yes – there is!
SITTAH: Who *is* this Daya?
RECHA: She's a Christian woman
Who looked after me when I was young –
Took care of me so well – you'd not believe!
I hardly missed my mother. God repay her!
Nonetheless, she terrified and tortured me!
SITTAH: But what about and why? How could she have?
RECHA: Poor woman! As I told you, she's a Christian;
She tortures out of love, a kindly zealot,
Who's convinced she knows the one true path
To God!
SITTAH: Now I begin to understand!
RECHA: She's one of those who therefore feel obliged
To take control of anyone who strays.
Nor can she help it, for, in fact, she's sure
Hers is the only path that leads aright.
How, then, could she calmly watch her friends
Veer off along a road that leads instead
To everlasting ruin and destruction?
She would have to love as well as hate
The self-same person at the self-same time!
That's not the only reason I'm compelled
At last to utter these complaints against her.
I'd gladly have continued to endure
Her sighs, her warnings, prayers, even threats
For often they induced thoughts good and useful.
Moreover, who does not at heart feel flattered,
Being held so dear and precious by another
That he or she just cannot bear the thought
Of losing one for all eternity!
SITTAH: Oh, how true!

RECHA: But things have gone too far!
   I've no resistance left, no patience nor
   The strength to ponder!
SITTAH: Ponder? What about?
RECHA: What she has only just disclosed to me.
SITTAH: Disclosed? And only now?
RECHA: This
   very hour!
   On our way here, we neared a tumbledown
   Christian chapel. Suddenly she stopped,
   Seeming to struggle with herself, then looked
   With tear-damp eyes, first heavenwards and then,
   Straight at myself and finally, she said:
   Come, let's take a short cut through the chapel!
   I followed her, eyeing the swaying ruins
   Nervously and then she stopped once more,
   And I could see the sunken steps that led
   To a rotting altar. Picture how I felt
   When Daya, wringing her hands, and shedding tears,
   Fell at my feet…
SITTAH: Oh, my dear child, what then?
RECHA: By the Holy Mother who must there have heard
   So many an anguished prayer and wrought so many
   Miracles, Daya implored me with a pleading look
   Of deep compassion to take pity on
   My loved ones or, at least, forgive her
   If perforce she now revealed the claim
   Upon me which her Christian faith must make –
SITTAH: (*Aside.*) Poor girl! I had begun to guess as much!
RECHA: That I was born of Christians and baptised:
   I was not Nathan's daughter, nor was he
   My father! God! Oh, God! He's not my father!
   Sittah, I'm at your feet once more!
SITTAH: No, Recha!
   No, no, stand up! My brother's coming! Rise!

Scene 7

SALADIN and the two as before.

SALADIN: What's going on here?
SITTAH: She's beside herself!
SALADIN: Who is it?
SITTAH: You know…
SALADIN: Is it Nathan's daughter?
     What ails her?
SITTAH: Child, control yourself! The Sultan…
RECHA: (*Sinks to her knees at Sultan's feet, forehead resting on the
     floor.*) I won't stand up! I can't. I'd sooner not
     Behold the Sultan's face – I would prefer
     Not to admire, reflected in his eyes
     And on his brow, that everlasting good
     And generous soul…
SALADIN: Stand up, child! Stand!
RECHA: Not till he promises…
SALADIN: I promise –
     Anything you like!
RECHA: No more nor less
     Than to allow me keep my father and
     Him me! I still have no idea who else
     Would or could desire to be my father.
     Nor do I want to know. Does blood alone –
     And nothing more – a father make?
SALADIN: (*Raising her to her feet.*)   I see…
     Who could have been so cruel to you, child –
     As to implant that notion in your head?
     Is it well-founded? Has the thing been proved?
RECHA: It must have been, for Daya says she had it
     From my nurse.
SALADIN: Your nurse?
RECHA: Who, at death's door,
     Felt duty bound at last to share the secret.
SALADIN: Dying? You don't think she was merely rambling?
     Even were it true, no – blood alone
     By no means makes a father – hardly would

It make the father of an animal.
At best, it could confer a prior right
To claim the title. But, fear not, my child.
Once two fathers start to fight for you,
Abandon both in favour of a third –
And take *me* for your father!

SITTAH: Oh, yes, do!

SALADIN: I'd be good – outstanding, as a father!
Hold! I've thought of something even better:
Why waste your time with fathers anyway?
What, when they come to die? You should
Be looking round for somebody to walk
In step with you through life? No-one in mind?

SITTAH: Don't make the poor girl blush!

SALADIN: I meant
her to.
A blush can make the ugly look enchanting;
How much more so one who's beautiful!
I've sent for your father – Nathan – and another:
Can you guess who? With your permission, Sittah!

SITTAH: Brother!

SALADIN: He'll make you blush and no mistake!

RECHA: Blush? Before whom?

SALADIN: You little hypocrite!
All right, turn pale – if that's what you prefer!
(*A female SLAVE enters and approaches SITTAH.*)
Surely they must be here by now? They are?

SITTAH: Good. Then send them in. Brother, it's they!

Scene 8

As before, with NATHAN and TEMPLAR.

SALADIN: Ah, my dear, good friends! Welcome, but first,
Nathan, I must tell you right away
That you may send a servant to take back
The money which you lent me recently.

NATHAN: Sire!

SALADIN: Moreover, I am at your service...
NATHAN: Sire!
SALADIN: The caravan's arrived and I am richer
    Now than I have been for ages past.
    Come, tell me what you need to undertake
    Some major project, something really grand!
    I know you merchants, too, can never have
    Too much ready cash in hand!
NATHAN: But why
    Discuss this trifle first? For don't I see
    A tearful eye more urgently in need
    Of my solicitude? (*Approaches RECHA.*)
                   Have you been weeping?
    What ails you? Are you not my daughter still?
RECHA:
    Father!
NATHAN: Enough, we understand each other!
    Be of good cheer! Calm down! Provided that
    Your heart is still your own, nor threatened
    With some other loss, don't fret. You have
    Not lost your father!
RECHA: There's no other threat!
TEMPLAR: No other, true? Then I've deceived myself.
    That which a man is not afraid of losing,
    He's never truly been convinced he owns
    Or wished to own. So much the better, Nathan!
    That alters everything completely! We,
    Saladin, are here at your behest,
    But I misled you. Fret your mind no more!
SALADIN: Over-hasty yet again, young man!
    Is everyone obliged to come your way
    And all of us be left to puzzle out
    Your meaning?
TEMPLAR: Sultan, you have heard, you've seen.
SALADIN: Indeed I have, young man and it's a pity
    That you were not more certain of your facts!
TEMPLAR: But now I am.
SALADIN: Who trades upon a deed
    Well done, cancels it out. That's why

The girl you saved is not your property.
Or else a thief who braved a fire
Impelled by greed, would be no less a hero
Than yourself.
(*Approaching RECHA, to lead her towards the
TEMPLAR.*)
                              Dear child, come over here!
Don't be too hard on him! Were he not so,
He'd be less warm, less proud; in short, he'd not
Have rescued you. Weigh one against the other!
Come, shame him into doing what, by right,
He ought to do: declare your love for him!
Woo him yourself! And if he should reject you
Or ever should forget how, by this step,
You've done far more for him than he for you...
All said and done, what did he do for you?
He let himself be slightly smoked, that's all!
And claims a right? If so, he's nothing like
My brother Assad! No, he wears his mask
But not his heart. Now, come, my dear!
SITTAH:
  Go, love!
It's little enough, so great your gratitude,
A trifle.
NATHAN: Saladin and Sittah, wait!
SALADIN: You, too?
NATHAN: Another voice has yet to speak.
SALADIN: Who says it shouldn't? Indisputably,
  A foster-father such as Nathan must
  Be heard. Speak first, if you so wish; I know
  In full how matters stand.
NATHAN: Not quite in full!
  I didn't mean myself, but someone else:
  A very different person, Saladin,
  But one to whom I beg you'll listen –
SALADIN: Who?
NATHAN: Her brother!
SALADIN: Recha's brother?
NATHAN: Yes!

RECHA:
> My brother?
> Have I a brother, then?

TEMPLAR: (*Shaken out of his distraught but silent reverie.*)
> Where is he? Where?
> This brother, it was he I came to meet.
> Isn't he here yet?

NATHAN: Patience!

TEMPLAR: (*Extremely bitter.*) He's already
> Foisted a father on her! Shouldn't be
> Too hard to find a brother!

SALADIN: That is all
> We needed! Christian, such a vile suspicion
> My brother Assad never would have voiced!
> Nathan, proceed! I ask you to forgive him!

NATHAN: I'll forgive him gladly for who knows
> What we'd have thought in his place, young as he?
> (*Approaching him in friendly fashion.*)
> Of course, Sir Knight, suspicion follows
> Swiftly from mistrust! If only you
> Had honoured me at once with your *true* name...

TEMPLAR:
> What?

NATHAN: You're no von Stauffen!

TEMPLAR: Then, what am I?

NATHAN: You're not Curd von Stauffen, anyway!

TEMPLAR: Then what's my name?

NATHAN: It's Leu von Filnek.

TEMPLAR: What?

NATHAN: You're flabbergasted?

TEMPLAR: Rightly! Who
> says that?

NATHAN: I do and I have more to tell you, though
> I'm not accusing you of lying...

TEMPLAR: Aren't you?

NATHAN: The second name could also well be yours.

TEMPLAR: How could I guess? (*Aside.*) God must be

> guiding him!

NATHAN: Your mother was a Stauffen, that's a fact.
  It was her brother, that's to say, your uncle,
  Who reared you, since your parents gave him charge
  Of you when driven by dire circumstance,
  Fled Germany, returning here once more.
  His name was Curd von Stauffen. He perhaps
  Adopted you as son instead of ward.
  How long is it since you came here with him?
  And is he still alive?
TEMPLAR: What shall I say?
  Nathan, you're correct. That's how it was.
  My uncle died, however. I came here
  With the Order's latest batch of reinforcements.
  I cannot see, though, what this has to do
  With Recha's brother.
NATHAN: Well, your father –
TEMPLAR: Did
  You know him? Him as well?
NATHAN: He was my friend.
TEMPLAR: Your friend? He could have been!
NATHAN:
        His name
  Was Wolf von Filnek, but he wasn't German.
TEMPLAR: You know that, too?
NATHAN: Just married to a German;
  He followed your mother to Germany, it's true,
  But didn't stay there long...
TEMPLAR: No more, I beg
  Of you! But Recha's brother? What of him?
NATHAN: You are he!
TEMPLAR: Her brother – I!?
RECHA:
  My brother?
SITTAH: Brother and sister!
SALADIN: Siblings!
RECHA: (*Moving towards him.*)   Oh, my brother!
TEMPLAR: (*Stepping back a pace.*)
  Her brother!
RECHA: (*Stands still and turns to NATHAN.*)
                No, it can't be true! Not true!

His heart knows nothing of it! We are fakes!

SALADIN: (*To the TEMPLAR.*)

Fakes? How so? What are you thinking of?
You are a fake, all right, for everything
About you's false! Your face, your voice, your gait!
Not to acknowledge such a sister! Go!

TEMPLAR: (*Approaching him humbly.*)

Don't you, too, misinterpret my amazement,
Sultan! Do not misjudge me and your brother,
Searching in vain for instant recognition
Of Assad in myself! (*Hurrying towards NATHAN.*)
                      You, Nathan, give
And take away – with both hands full! But no!
You've given me far, far more than you have taken!
(*Embracing RECHA.*)
Recha, my sister! Oh, my sister, Recha!

NATHAN: Blanda von Filnek.

TEMPLAR: Blanda? Recha – no?

Recha is yours no longer? You reject her?
You give her back her Christian name for me!
For my sake, you are doing this? Oh, Nathan!
Why make her pay for all of this? My sister!

NATHAN: Pay? Oh, children, children! Can't you see?
Will not my daughter's brother equally
Become my child, the moment that he wishes?
(*Leaving them to their embraces, SALADIN, astonished
and uneasy, walks over to SITTAH.*)

SALADIN: What say you, sister?

SITTAH: I am deeply moved.

SALADIN: And I, my dear, am almost shuddering
At thought of something even more affecting
Prepare yourself for it as best you can.

SITTAH: What's
that?

SALADIN: Nathan, we must have a word!
(*While NATHAN approaches him, SITTAH joins the
brother and sister to demonstrate her sympathy and
NATHAN and SALADIN lower their voices.*)

SALADIN: Listen Nathan, listen! Weren't you saying
  Her father didn't come from Germany;
  At least, not German-born. So what was he?
  Where did he hail from?
NATHAN: That he never did
  Confide to me. Nor ever gave a hint.
SALADIN: He wasn't Frankish? Not a westerner?
NATHAN: That much he did admit, I do recall.
  He liked best speaking Persian.
SALADIN: Persian?
  What more is needed? He it is – or was!
NATHAN: Who?
SALADIN: My brother, Assad! Him for sure!
  I am convinced!
NATHAN: Then, since you say so,
  Take this book as further confirmation.
  (*Handing him the breviary.*)
SALADIN: (*Opening it eagerly.*)
  That's his writing! I can tell at once!
NATHAN: They're in the dark still, so it's up to you
  How much you feel disposed to let them know!
SALADIN: (*Aside, while leafing through the book.*)
  Should I not recognise my brother's children?
  My nieces and my nephews, as *my* children?
  Not recognise them? Leave them all to you?
  (*Aloud.*) That's what they are, Sittah! Both of them!
  They're mine and yours! The children of our brother.
  (*Runs to embrace them.*)
SITTAH: (*Following him.*) I hear aright? Could it be otherwise!
SALADIN: (*To TEMPLAR.*)
  Now, you stubborn man, you'll have to love me!
  (*To RECHA.*) Am I not what I offered you just now?
  Whether or not you like it!
SITTAH: Me as well!
SALADIN: (*Returning to the TEMPLAR.*)
  My son! My Assad! You're my Assad's son!
TEMPLAR: I share your blood! So then the dreams
  That rocked my childhood cradle were, in fact,

Much more than dreams! (*Kneeling at his feet.*)
SALADIN:
(*Raising him to his feet.*)   Look at the scallywag!
Something of this he knew and yet he could
Have very well made me his murderer!
(*Curtain falls amid mutual embraces.*)

The End.